W9-AGJ-972

THE

CAYMAN
ISLANDS
ALIVE!

THE

CAYMAN ISLANDS

ALIVE!

Paris Permenter & John Bigley

HUNTER

HUNTER PUBLISHING, INC.
130 Campus Drive, Edison, NJ 08818
732-225-1900; 800-255-0343; Fax 732-417-1744
hunterp@bellsouth.net

1220 Nicholson Road, Newmarket, Ontario
Canada L3Y 7V1
800-399-6858; Fax 800-363-2665

The Boundary, Wheatley Road, Garsington
Oxford, OX44 9EJ England
01865-361122; Fax 01865-361133

ISBN 1-55650-862-X
© 1999 Paris Permenter & John Bigley

Maps by K. André © 1999 Hunter Publishing, Inc.

3   4

About The Authors

John Bigley and Paris Permenter fell in love with the Caribbean over a dozen years ago and have turned their extensive knowledge of the region into an occupation. As professional travel writers and photographers, the pair contribute travel articles and photographs on the US and the Caribbean to many national consumer and trade publications. The husband-and-wife team have also written numerous guidebooks.

Paris and John are authors of several other Hunter guidebooks, including *Adventure Guide to the Cayman Islands, Adventure Guide to the Leeward Islands* and *Jamaica: A Taste of the Island*. Currently they're at work on *Jamaica Alive!, Nassau & The Best of The Bahamas Alive!, Antigua, Barbuda, St. Kitts & Nevis Alive!,* and *Adventure Guide to Jamaica.*

Paris and John are also frequent television and radio talk show guests on the subject of travel. Both are members of the prestigious Society of American Travel Writers (SATW) and the American Society of Journalists and Authors (ASJA).

When they're not on the road, the team resides in the Texas Hill Country near Austin.

More about Paris and John's work can be found on their website: www.parisandjohn.com.

www.hunterpublishing.com

Hunter's full range of travel guides to all corners of the globe is featured on our exciting website. You'll find guidebooks to suit every type of traveler, no matter what their budget, lifestyle, or idea of fun. Full descriptions are given for each book, along with reviewers' comments and a cover image. Books may be purchased on-line using a credit card via our secure transaction system.

Check out our *Adventure Guides*, a series aimed at the independent traveler with a focus on outdoor activities (rafting, hiking, biking, skiing, etc.). All books in this signature series cover places to stay and eat, sightseeing, in-town attractions, transportation and more!

Hunter's *Romantic Weekends* series offers myriad things to do for couples of all ages and lifestyles. Quaint places to stay and restaurants where the ambiance will take your breath away are included, along with fun activities that you and your partner will remember forever.

About the Alive Guides

Reliable, detailed and personally researched by knowledgeable authors, the Alive series was founded by Harriet and Arnold Greenberg.

This accomplished travel-writing team also operates a renowned bookstore, **The Complete Traveller**, at 199 Madison Avenue in New York City.

Other titles in this series include:

* ❈ Antigua, Barbuda, St. Kitts & Nevis
* ❈ Aruba, Bonaire & Curaçao
* ❈ Bermuda
* ❈ Buenos Aires & The Best of Argentina
* ❈ Cancún & Cozumel
* ❈ Jamaica
* ❈ Martinique, Guadeloupe, Dominica & St. Lucia
* ❈ Nassau & The Best of The Bahamas
* ❈ St. Martin & St. Barts
* ❈ Venezuela
* ❈ The Virgin Islands

We Love to Get Mail

This book has been carefully researched to bring you current, accurate information. But no place is unchanging. We welcome your comments for future editions. Please write us at: *The Cayman Islands Alive*, c/o Hunter Publishing, 130 Campus Drive, Edison, NJ 08818, or e-mail your comments to kimba@ mediasoft.net.

Contents

Maps

Introduction

Ready, set, go!

Whether you're a certified diver or a non-swimmer, the Cayman Islands are the place for you to act out your fantasies. If that means scuba diving à la Jacques Cousteau, shopping 'til you drop for baubles from around the globe, mingling with the jetset crowd at a luxurious resort, or just finding a quiet piece of sand to call your own for the day, these islands have got you covered.

Just over an hour's flight from Miami and less than two hours from Houston, the Cayman Islands are one of the easiest Caribbean destinations to reach. That easy access – combined with a high standard of living, low level of crime, and plenty of sun and sand – continues to draw record number of travelers. Many come again and again, and some returnees even invest in their own slice of paradise with one of the many condominiums located here. Others choose the islands, one of the top banking capitals in the world, as a base for their businesses and corporations.

Grand Cayman is 480 miles south of Miami & 150 miles south of Cuba.

★ DID YOU KNOW?

Although it's often called "the Caymans," technically there is no such place. It's either "Cayman" or "Cayman Islands."

Often just referred to as "Cayman," this destination is actually three distinct islands. **Grand Cayman**, the showy big brother, is home to most of the tourism industry as well as the banking industry. The Sister Islands of **Cayman Brac** and **Little Cayman**, each favored by scuba divers as well as anglers (and those looking to get away from it all), are located about 80 miles east-northeast of Grand Cayman and are separated from each other by seven miles of ocean. Cayman Brac covers about 14 square miles and Little Cayman, 10 square miles.

Whatever island you select, you'll be happy. Grab some sunscreen and make your way to this luxurious destination where peddling is prohibited, and the living is definitely easy.

The Attractions

The Cayman Islands keep drawing vacationers again and again – in spite of an exchange rate that's not in Americans' favor. The secret of these little islands? Here's our analysis of the reasons you, like 373,000 air travelers and 771,000 cruise passengers last year, might consider a vacation in the Cayman Islands:

The average household income on the islands is CI $56,000 (US $68,292). The islands have a low unemployment rate.

- ❆ Great weather
- ❆ World-class scuba diving
- ❆ Duty-free shopping
- ❆ Easy access
- ❆ High level of safety
- ❆ Numerous angling opportunities
- ❆ Luxurious accommodations
- ❆ Fine dining
- ❆ A familiar atmosphere

So which island do you visit? These islands aren't identical triplets – they each have their own distinct personality, one that you'll want to match to your own. If you are interested in duty-free shopping, gourmet dining, and luxurious accommodations (either hotels, condominiums, or villas), make Grand Cayman your base.

If, on the other hand, you plan to spend most of your time looking for that secluded strip of sand where you never see another set of footprints, then Little Cayman should be your destination. This tiny island reaches just 40 feet above sea level at its highest point and is home to fewer than 100 residents. It's little changed from a century ago, a perfect place to get away from it all and spend your day on a bicycle peddling empty roads, snorkeling in pristine waters, or looking for that perfect beach.

To sound like a local, pronounce the largest island's name as "cay-MAN," with an emphasis on the last syllable.

If you are interested in watersports activity, you've got a tougher choice. Each of these islands is great for scuba divers, each well known in the world of diving. Bonefishing is also a top draw, especially on Little Cayman and Cayman Brac. Here you'll also find caving, birdwatching, and plenty of places for quiet walks.

❖ **TIP**

Whichever your choice, you're never limited to just one destination in the Cayman Islands. Island-hopping is easy! These isles are much smaller than their easterly neighbors such as Cuba and Jamaica, so don't choose only one area to explore – choose several!

The Alive Price Scale

Prices change as quickly as the sand shifts on a Caribbean beach. For that reason we've strayed away from providing dollar-and-cents figures. Besides the constantly changing prices, accommodations offer a wide variety of steps in their price scale as well: partial ocean view, full ocean view, oceanside, garden view – the list goes on and on. Each has its own price based on the month and the day of the week; when you make your reservation ask about all the categories.

For accommodations, our price scale is designed to give you a ballpark figure for a typical stay during peak season (December 15-April 15). We've based these estimates on a standard room for two persons. These figures don't take into account additional amenities such as meal plans, dive packages, etc. Prices are given in US dollars.

Alive Price Scale - Accommodations

Deluxe	$300+
Expensive	$200-$300
Moderate	$100-$200
Inexpensive	Under $100

6 ❖ *Introduction*

Be sure to conserve water during your stay. Fresh water is a precious commodity here.

All our hotel selections take major credit cards, are air-conditioned and have private baths, except in the case of the few guest houses where noted.

For dining, we've set up a price scale based on a three-course dinner, including appetizer or soup, an entrée, dessert and coffee. Cocktails and wine are extra. Price estimates are per person in US dollars.

Alive Price Scale - Restaurants

Expensive . . . . $40+

Moderate . . . . $25-$40

Inexpensive . . . . Under $25

For attractions, we've indicated which charge admission and which are free.

A Capsule History

Recorded Caymanian history begins, not with Grand Cayman, but with the Sister Islands of Cayman Brac and Little Cayman. These islands were spotted by Christopher Columbus on his last journey to the New World on May 10, 1503. The explorer was actually on his way from Panama to Hispaniola (now home of the Dominican Republic and Haiti), when he was blown off

course, a detour that brought him within sight
of the Sister Islands.

Columbus named these islands "Las Tortugas"
after the many sea turtles he found here. Later
maps referred to the islands as Lagartos, probably a reference to the large lizards (possibly
iguanas) seen on the island. Later, the name
became "Caymanas" from the Carib Indian
word for caymans, the marine crocodile.

⭐ **DID YOU KNOW?**

On a 1585 voyage, Sir Francis
Drake reported sighting "great
serpents called Caymanas, large
like lizards, which are edible."

A few years later, a French map showed
Cayman Brac with crocodiles in its waters and
a manuscript described the reptiles. There's no
need for modern visitors to worry about those
toothy lizards. In 1993 an archeological dig did
discover the skeleton of one on Grand Cayman,
followed by another three years later on
Cayman Brac, proving the existence of the crocodiles. But no living version has been spotted.

⭐ **DID YOU KNOW?**

Turtles are still a symbol of
Cayman: the unofficial mascot
is "Sir Turtle," a peg-legged,
swashbuckling turtle. The turtle even appears on the
Cayman Islands flag.

Turtles drew sailors to the region for years in an attempt to prevent scurvy. Their ships visited the islands, slaughtered and salted the turtles to feed the crew.

Slowly, human population rose and the first royal land grant in Grand Cayman came in 1734, marking the first permanent settlement. Through 1800, the population continued to grow with the arrival of shipwrecked mariners and immigrants from Jamaica. Cayman Brac and Little Cayman remained primarily uninhabited, visited only by turtle hunters during season (some records show the tiny islands were settled but residents were attacked by pirates).

For years, the Cayman Islands served as a magnet for pirates. Buccaneers such as Sir Henry Morgan enjoyed its sunny shores for at least brief stopovers. During the American Revolution, American privateers challenged English shipping, aided by the war ships and merchant ships of France, Spain, and Holland. By 1782, peace came to the seas and buccaneering drew to a close.

In 1832 the citizens of the Cayman Islands met at what is today the oldest remaining structure on the island: St. James Castle. Remembered as the "Birthplace of Democracy" in Cayman, this site witnessed the first vote to create a legislature of representatives.

Wreck of the Ten Sails

According to research, in 1794, a great maritime tragedy took place on Grand Cayman. "The Wreck of the Ten Sails" is legendary, recalling the tragedy of the *Cordelia*, part of a convoy of merchant ships headed to Britain from Jamaica. *Cordelia* ran aground on the reef at the East End and frantically sent a signal to the other ships to warn them off the dangerous coral. Sadly, the signal was misunderstood and, one by one, the tall ships sailed into the reef. Residents of East End were credited for their quick actions that left no life unsaved, an act that King George III later recognized. Various stories explain that King George III granted the islands freedom from conscription and other versions say that the king gave the islands freedom from taxation.

By 1835, slavery had been outlawed by Great Britain and the islands led a quiet existence, many of the population working as turtle fishermen or building turtling boats. The sea provided a livelihood for most residents, who then traded for agricultural items that couldn't be grown on the island. Palm thatch was transformed into marine rope and offered a good barter for daily staples. During this time, shipbuilding became a major industry as well. (Palm thatch played such an important role in Cayman's history it even appears on the Caymanian flag.)

The Islands Today

For the next century, the Cayman Islands remained relatively isolated. Residents continued their old traditions but hurricanes, tidal waves, and a depletion of the green turtle supply forced some residents to sail to Cuba, Honduras, and Nicaragua to earn a living. The merchant seamen navigated the waters and this sustained the economy of the islands until tourism and finance rose to prominence in the 20th century. During this time the islands were cut off geographically and lacked much communication with the outside world. The first wireless station wasn't built until 1935.

The plunge into the 20th century was aided by commissioner Sir Allen Cardinall, who served from 1934 to 1940. Linking the public buildings of Grand Cayman with a network of roads, the commissioner was also the first public figure to recognize the tourism potential of the islands, even noting that this area held "the most perfect bathing beaches in the West Indies." In 1953, the first airfield in the Cayman Islands was completed with the Owens Roberts Airport on Grand Cayman. A year later, an airstrip opened on Cayman Brac. Within three years tourism began taking hold on Seven Mile Beach, Grand Cayman. By 1957, dive operator Bob Soto began the islands' first recreational diving business and introduced the world to these pristine waters.

The islands continued as a dependency of Jamaica, both under the protectorate of Great Britain until 1962 when Jamaica became independent. The Caymanians had a far different view of the Union Jack than their Jamaican neighbors, however; in 1962 a vote overwhelmingly favored remaining a British dependency.

★ DID YOU KNOW?

These islands are a dependent territory or a British Crown Colony of the UK. They are led by the Governor, an appointee of the Queen. The Governor leads the Executive Council, which includes three official and four elected members. The unicameral legislature consists of 15 members. The government offices are on Elgin Street in George Town.

He Hath Founded It Upon The Seas

The motto of the Cayman Islands, "He hath founded it upon the seas," describes this destination perfectly. The sea is an integral part of life here, both for residents and vacationers. And it is never more than a short distance away, no matter where you are on the islands.

The People

The three Cayman Islands boast a total population of just over 35,600, with the bulk of those residents found on Grand Cayman. About 34,280 people reside on the largest island, followed by 1,200 residents on Cayman Brac and a scant 120 people on Little Cayman.

It's a varied population, with cultures from around the globe. About a third of all residents are non-Caymanians. Most are from the US, Canada, the UK and nearby Jamaica, although a total of 113 nationalities are represented.

Environment

These islands are low and fairly dry, especially when compared to neighboring Jamaica. On Grand Cayman, the elevation is only about 60 feet above sea level at its highest point. The Sister Islands are each amoebae-shaped and small. Cayman Brac soars to a nosebleed level, by Caymanian standards, of 140 feet above sea level.

To sound like a local resident, pronounce Brac as "braCK," with a hard ending.

These three islands are actually the peaks of a submarine mountain range, the Cayman Ridge, part of a chain running from Cuba to near Belize. The islands are actually limestone outcroppings with little soil, so vegetation is not as lush as on some islands.

The islands are covered with two types of limestone: bluff limestone, formed about 30 million years ago, and ironshore, a substance created about 120,000 years ago, combining limestone with coral, mollusk shell, and marl. Ironshore accounts for the pocked surface that holds little pockets of soil (and makes walking barefoot just about impossible) on much of these islands.

You won't hear us complaining about the rough ground that makes up these islands, though. The limestone and little soil means that there's very little runoff. The result? Crystal-clear waters directly offshore.

Flora

The Cayman Islands are not as lush as neighboring Jamaica but still boast a good variety of tropical flora and fauna. The **wild banana orchid** is the national flower, selected from among 27 indigenous orchid species. Blooming in April and May, it is found on all three islands in different varieties. In all, 26 species of orchids are found on the islands, five found nowhere else.

The national tree is the **silver thatch palm**. The palm has a silvery underside with light green upper fronds. For all its beauty, this plant has far more than ornamental value, though. It has been used by islanders to form roofing, belts, baskets, rope, and more. Palm rope has long been a bartering tool, traded for staples.

The **mango** is the most plentiful fruit in the Cayman Islands, ripening in the month of June and continuing to produce through September. The islands harvest about 65,000 pounds of this tropical treasure every season. There are 15 different varieties of mango; you'll find it at roadside stands and farmers' markets.

Fauna

Animals & Reptiles

The Cayman Islands don't have a lot of wildlife, but there are some small animals that can be seen.

A shy resident of these islands is the **agouti**, a rabbit-sized rodent once hunted for meat. Introduced by the early settlers, the agouti is a Central American native. Once kept as a pet and raised for food, today the rodent is rarely seen in the wild. A family of agoutis can be viewed at the Cayman Turtle Farm on Grand Cayman. The agouti has long, thin legs, hoof-like claws with three toes on its hind feet and five toes on its forefeet.

The **hickatee**, a freshwater turtle, is found in the freshwater and brackish ponds in the Cayman Islands and neighboring Cuba.

Although the Cayman Islands have no poisonous snakes, you might spot one of the harmless indigenous species such as the **grass snake**. The numbers of this snake, which feeds on frogs and lizards, have been reduced by the **mongoose**, which was introduced to control rats. (Unfortunately, rats and mongoose keep different hours, so the mongoose feed on the snake – the natural predator of the rat – causing the rat population to swell.)

A favorite sighting is that of the **blue iguana**, a vegetarian species that can grow to a length of five feet.

The blue iguana is often seen sunning itself (sometimes in the middle of the road).

Little Cayman is home to over 2,000 iguanas (check out the "iguana crossing" signs around the island). On Grand Cayman, you can see a large male on display in the Queen Elizabeth II Botanic Gardens.

Birds

Birdlovers flock to these islands to see parrots, ducks, cuckoos, herons, and other species. One of the most exotic species is the national bird, the **Cayman parrot**.

You might hear the Cayman parrot's call even before you see its iridescent green feathers.

Look for these birds in early mornings and late afternoons when they return to roost in the stumps of palm trees. (Sadly there are no parrots on Little Cayman. That bird population disappeared in 1932 with the Great Hurricane and never returned.) These parrots eat fruit, flowers and seeds in the dry woodlands.

Another commonly seen bird is the **Zenaida dove**, a cooing dove that feeds on dried seeds. The colorful **bananaquit**, a yellow and black bird that's not shy about begging for crumbs (and its favorite treat: sugar) is another common sight.

Red-footed boobies are easily sighted on Little Cayman. Here you'll find 7,000 boobies, about 30% of the Caribbean population of this species. This beige bird, about 25 inches long, nests high in the trees. Its young are pure white. Boobies construct a rough nest of sticks that's easy to spot.

Magnificent frigate birds are also sighted in these islands. With a wingspan of over seven feet and wings sharply angled like boomerangs, the black frigate bird is fairly easy to spot as it soars high over the sea.

Frigate birds are aggressive to others. They often hit the red-footed booby in flight in an attempt to make it disgorge its meal and provide an easy dinner for itself.

Little Cayman in particular is a favorite with birders, who come to the tiny isle for the chance to spot red footed boobies, magnificent frigate birds, West Indian whistling ducks, cattle egrets, black necked stilts, snowy egrets, tricoloured herons, and others. Cayman Brac is favored for its parrot viewing, with a large reserve dedicated to these colorful birds. Grand Cayman is also home to several protected areas and ponds where both migrating and resident birds thrive.

Life Undersea

For travelers, these islands are a destination sought for their underwater attractions, with many of the best dive sites on the globe, waters with a clarity second to none, a diversity of dives to interest even the most jaded diver, and a variety of marine life that can't be beat. Vacations here spend a lot of time in those crystalline waters. Divers and snorkelers will find marine playgrounds around each of the islands. Fishermen wrestle wily bonefish in the shallow flats or struggle with blue marlin, yellowfin tuna, or wahoo from deep-water charter boats. Those looking for a more leisurely pace enjoy sunset sails or long walks along powdery beaches.

The **green sea turtle** is an integral part of Cayman culture and a symbol of these islands. Even in their current protected state, only one turtle out of 10,000 eggs laid reaches maturity. The turtles are threatened by birds, animals, marine life, and, of course, humans. Even so, the turtle has continued to thrive in Cayman waters.

★ **DID YOU KNOW?**
Green sea turtles can stay underwater for several days without surfacing for air.

The Cayman Islands have taken strict measures to protect the marine life of these waters. Today the sea turtle is protected and no one may disturb, molest, or take turtles in Cayman waters without a license.

Each of the Cayman Islands is surrounded by coral reefs, producing some of the best snorkeling and scuba diving in the Caribbean. Divers have a chance at spotting a wide array of marine life, partly because of the deep water located nearby. The **Cayman Trough**, the deepest waters in the Caribbean, lies between this nation and Jamaica, with depths that plunge into inky blackness over four miles beneath the ocean's surface.

✷ WARNING!

Whenever you are snorkeling or diving, watch out for fire coral. There are many varieties, all edged with white. If you accidentally brush against the coral it will defend itself and burn you like fire!

Climate

Usually the weather in these islands can be summed up in one word: perfect. Blessed with cooling trade winds, the Cayman Islands enjoy a temperate climate year-round. You'll find the temperatures warm enough to enjoy a dip in the sea all year through, but cool enough to encourage you to get out and explore the island, stroll George Town for a few hours of shopping, and dine outside comfortably. There's no need to run from an air-conditioned car to an air-conditioned hotel lobby on these islands.

The coolest month is February. July and August are the hottest, with highs approaching 90° (although high humidity levels can make it feel much warmer).

CLIMATE CHART		
Month	Temperature (°F; low/high)	Rainfall (inches)
January	75/83	3.1
February	74/83	1.3
March	75/85	0.8
April	77/86	0.8
May	77/87	3.1
June	78/87	6.7
July	77/87	9.2
August	78/88	3.7
September	78/88	6.2
October	77/87	9.2
November	75/85	7.9
December	74/83	5.2

Water temperatures vary slightly during the winter months. In the cooler season, the sea ranges from 78 to 82°, rising about 5° during the summer months.

Rainfall varies with the seasons. Generally, rainstorms are heavy but brief. The islands receive about 46 inches of precipitation annually. The driest times are March and April.

Hurricanes

Mention weather and the Caribbean in the same sentence and, quite predictably, the topic of hurricanes arises. These deadly storms are officially a threat from June through November, although the greatest danger is during the later months, basically August through October (September is the worst).

You'll find a list of hurricane shelters in the Cable and Wireless telephone directory.

Hurricanes are defined as revolving storms with wind speeds of 75 mph or greater. These counterclockwise storms begin as waves off the west coast of Africa and work their way across the Atlantic, some eventually gaining strength and becoming tropical depressions (under 40 mph) or tropical storms (40-74 mph). Excellent warning systems keep islanders posted on the possibility of oncoming storms. Radio Cayman broadcasts current storm reports in the islands.

Keep in mind, however, that the Caribbean is a large region. We were on Grand Cayman when Hurricane Luis picked up strength on its way to batter St. Martin and Antigua in 1995 and never saw surf over ankle high.

Want to check out today's forecast? Have a look at the weather page (www.caymanislands.ky).

Getting There ✈

By Air

Most air travelers arrive in the Cayman Islands at Grand Cayman's **Owen Roberts International Airport**, a modern facility that includes a tourist board desk with brochures and maps as well as, for your return, plenty of duty-free shopping. The airport received a substantial facelift just a few years ago to enlarge and improve all the visitor areas as well as baggage claim and customs. The airport is served by over 100 flights per week.

Departure tax is US $12.50 per person; no tax is charged for inter-island travel.

Cayman Airways (☎ 800/G-CAYMAN or 345/949-2311). The national carrier offers flights from Miami (three daily), Tampa, Orlando, and Houston. Flights to Grand Cayman from Miami average about 70 minutes.

American Airlines (☎ 800/433-7300). American has direct service to Grand Cayman from Miami (and Raleigh-Durham during high season).

Northwest Airlines (☎ 800/225-2525). North-west offers flights from Detroit, Miami and Tampa.

USAirways International (☎ 800/447-4747) has service from Charlotte and Tampa.

Delta (☎ 800/325-1999) offers daily 767 service between Atlanta and Grand Cayman.

Air Jamaica (☎ 800/523-5585) has regular ser-vice to Kingston, Jamaica with connecting ser-vice to Montego Bay as well as several Caribbean islands.

British Airways (☎ 800/247-9297) has twice-weekly service from London. In addition, it runs three weekly DC-10 flights from London (Gatwick) to Grand Cayman on Monday, Wednesday and Friday with an intermediate stop in Nassau, Bahamas.

★ DID YOU KNOW?

Low-cost flights to Grand Cayman can be obtained through charter companies during high season. Ask your travel agent to check with char-ter and tour companies offering air-only and air-land packages.

Coming from Europe or Asia

Although three out of four Cayman Islands visi-tors come from the United States, the European market makes up a significant segment of arrivals. Nearly 22,000 vacationers arrived from the UK, followed by over 11,000 from Europe and nearly 1,200 from Japan. Regardless of the home base, the target market for the Cayman Islands remains the same: "affluent travelers with a sense of adventure," according to Jonathan Sloan, Senior Account Manager with McCluskey & Associates, the London-based public relations firm of the Cayman Islands.

UK tour operators include Airtours, Airwaves, American Connection, Barefoot Traveller, British Airways Holidays, Caribbean Connection, Caribtours, Elegant Resorts, Getaway Vacations, Goldenjoy Holidays, Harlequin Worldwide Travel, Hayes and Jarvis, International Charters, Key to America, Kuoni, North America Travel Service, Regal Holidays, Scuba Safaris, Seligo, Sport Abroad, Sunworld Beach Villas, Thomas Cook Holidays, Tradewinds, Virgin Holidays, and Worldwide Fishing Safaris. "The list for US and European wholesalers is quite extensive and includes all the major recognized wholesalers," says Sloan.

The Cayman Department of Tourism Frankfurt office works with a variety of tour operators, including Aeroworld GMBH, Airtours International, Blue Marine International Reisen GMBH, Dertour Deutsches Reisenbuero, Karibik Inside, Terraplan Karibik, Airturs Austria, Meine Reise, Poncho Tours, Travac Austria, Carib Tours, Imholz Resen AG, Kuoni Reisen, and others.

Overseas Tourism Offices

In the UK

Cayman Islands Tourism
6 Arlington Street
London, SW1A 1RE, England
☎ 0171-491-7771, fax 0171-409-7773

Germany/Austria/Switzerland

Marketing Services International
Walter Stoehrer and Partner GmbH
Johanna-Melber-Weg 12
D-60599 Frankfurt, Germany
☎ 069-60-320-94, fax 069-62-92-64

Italy

G & A Martinengo
Via Fratelli Ruffini 9, 20 123 Milano, Italy
☎ 02-4801-2068, fax 02-635-32

Spain

Sergat España SL
Pau Casals 4, 08021 Barcelona, Spain
☎ 93-414-0210, fax 93-201-8657

France/Scandinavia

KPMG Axe Consultants
12 Rue De Madrid, 75005 Paris, France
☎ 33-1-53-424136, fax 33-1-43-873285

Argentina

Reitur, Representaciones Int'l Turisticas
Esmeralda 847 Piso Of. "F"
(1007) Buenos Aires, Argentina
☎ 54-1-315-0485, fax 54-1-315-0038

By Cruise Ship

Grand Cayman limits the number of cruise ships in port at any one time to three or four, with a maximum capacity of 6,000 passengers. This limit ensures that visitors have a good experience while on the island and never feel overcrowded in George Town.

Cruise ship arrivals are at an all-time high, rising 12% in the last year alone.

❋ TIP

Tuesday, Wednesday and Thursday are generally the busiest days for cruise ships in George Town. To avoid crowds, hit the beach or other attractions on those days.

Grand Cayman is served by numerous cruise lines, including Norwegian, Princess, Regal, Royal Caribbean, Royal, Sun Line, Carnival, Celebrity, Costa, Crystal, Crown Commodore, Cunard, Dolphin, Holland America, and many others.

Cruise ship passengers arrive by tender in George Town at either the North or South terminal (just steps apart). These terminals are located right in the heart of George Town, just a stroll from shopping and dining. The clean waterfront brims with shops featuring fine jewelry, black coral, artwork, leather goods, and other goodies.

Cruise visitors arriving for the day will find plenty of drivers just steps from the cruise terminals. These "guides" offer trips to Seven Mile Beach as well as island tours. You'll find plenty of organized tours (typically to the Turtle Farm, Hell, and Seven Mile Beach). To experience the island without the rush of a crowd, consider hiring a driver by the hour. A taxi stand is located at the terminal and a knowledgeable driver will take up to four persons for US $37.50 per hour.

If you'd rather spend your time on the beach, take a taxi directly to Seven Mile Beach, located about three miles from town. Taxi fare runs about US $4 per person each way; a steady flow of taxis from the hotels to town insures that you'll have no difficulty returning to the ship before departure time.

Inter-Island Travel

Many travelers, especially those returning to Grand Cayman, spend at least a day or two exploring the Sister Islands of Cayman Brac and Little Cayman. Although the distance is too far to be covered by ferry, inter-island flights are relatively inexpensive and easy to arrange.

Flights are available through **Island Air** (☎ 800/9-CAYMAN, 345/949-5252, fax 345/949-7044; e-mail iair@candw.ky) with scheduled twice-daily service between Grand Cayman, Little Cayman and Cayman Brac. Flight time is about 45 minutes. Rates start at just over US $100 for a day trip leaving from Grand Cayman.

Getting Ready

When to Visit

The peak (read: most expensive) time to visit the Cayman Islands is mid-December through mid-April. This is the busiest time of year, a season when Americans and Canadians are looking for a warm weather refuge, if only for a few days, and when hotels and condominiums can charge their highest rates.

> **⚠ WARNING!**
>
> Grand Cayman is also a spring break destination for many college students so, unless you enjoy a serious party atmosphere, avoid late March and early April. Spring breakers don't hit Little Cayman and Cayman Brac so these islands maintain their peaceful atmosphere year around.

You'll find equally pleasant weather conditions in the "shoulder" seasons – fall and spring. Prices are somewhat lower during these months and reservations are easier to obtain.

In the fall months, the busiest time is late October when the annual Pirates Week blowout fills hotels with merrymakers.

Early summer is an especially pleasant time to visit.

Summer months are the cheapest – look for rooms at 40-50% off their peak rates.

Late summer can bring the threat of hurricanes but it's a minor threat. Good forecasting systems keep travelers aware of any impending storms days in advance.

 Entry Requirements

US and Canadian citizens need to show proof of citizenship in the form of a passport, or other proof of citizenship such as a birth certificate. Visitors must also show a return airline ticket.

Travelers can remain in the islands for up to six months; to extend your visit you must obtain permission by writing the Chief Immigration Officer, Department of Immigration, P.O. Box 1098, Grand Cayman. On-island, the immigration offices are found at the Government Administration Building on Elgin Avenue in George Town.

Visas are not required of citizens from member countries of the Commonwealth or from Andorra, Austria, Belgium, Denmark, Finland, France, Germany, Greece, Iceland, Irish Republic, Italy, Japan, Liechtenstein, Luxembourg, Malta, Monaco, Netherlands, Norway, Portugal, San Marino, Spain, Sweden, and Switzerland.

Visitors can be refused entry if their appearance or behavior do not meet "normal" social standards.

Customs

US Customs

The Cayman Islands are a duty-free port, so after 48 hours out of the States, Americans can return home with up to US $400 in purchases without paying duty. (Families can pool their exemptions; a husband and wife can take an exemption of $800, a family of four $1,600.)

Cayman crafts are exempt from this allowance, as are works of art, caviar, foreign language books, and truffles.

✳ TIP

Turtle products – shells, steaks, lotion, and shell jewelry – sold on the island cannot be brought back into the US or through the US in transit to other countries. Skip these items at the Cayman Turtle Farm gift shop.

Each visitor can return with one carton of cigarettes and two liters of alcohol (only those visitors age 21 and over). Additional liquor purchases result in a duty approximately 15% above the duty-free cost.

Cuban cigars can legally be enjoyed while in the Cayman Islands, but cannot be brought back into the United States.

❋ TIP

Before your trip, get a copy of the *Know Before You Go* brochure (Publication 512) from the US Customs Service at your airport or by writing the US Customs Service, PO Box 7407, Washington, DC 20044.

Canadian Customs

If you are a Canadian citizen, you can return home with CI $300 in goods duty free if you have been away from Canada for seven days or longer (see page 37 for exchange rates). This exemption is good once per year. If you've been away more than 48 hours, you can claim an additional exemption of CI $100 per calendar quarter. (You can't claim the yearly and the quarterly exemptions within the same quarter.)

What to Pack

We're happy to say that you won't need to pack a steamer trunk for a vacation in the Cayman Islands. No matter what your planned activities, you'll find that these are casual islands. Unlike some other Caribbean islands which recall a more proper British standard of dress especially during high season, Cayman adheres to American standards of casual comfort, due in a large part to the high number of American ex-pats that now call this land home.

Shorts and t-shirts are the uniform of these islands. Be sure to bring along at least two swimsuits (the high humidity means that clothing takes extra time to dry). Swimwear is appropriate only for the beach, so you will want a cover-up, no matter how casual, for lunches and quick excursions.

Evenings are relaxed too. We've worn shorts and sandals to many al fresco restaurants on these islands. There are some establishments on Grand Cayman where you'll feel more comfortable in long pants, a collared shirt, or a simple dress; we've indicated these in the text.

Nightlife is also laid-back – leave the sequined dress for a trip to San Juan or Aruba. Sundresses, polo shirts, and sandals are seen in the islands' nightclubs and comedy clubs; most evening activity, however, takes place in the beach bars, where you'll feel most at home in those shorts once again.

Here's a brief checklist for all Cayman visitors:

- ❏ *Proof of citizenship*
- ❏ *Airline tickets*
- ❏ *Snorkel, fins, and mask*
- ❏ *Sunscreen*
- ❏ *Aloe vera gel*

❑ *First aid kit*

❑ *Cameras, flash and film (we recommend an inexpensive underwater camera too)*

❑ *Drivers license for car rental*

❑ *Swimsuit*

❑ *All prescriptions (in original bottles)*

❑ *Mini-address book*

If you're considering a boat excursion, bring along non-skid shoes.

If you'll be scuba diving, don't forget your "C" card as well as any gear you typically bring along: compass, dive tables, dive computer, weight belt, mesh bag, dive boots, logbook, and proof of insurance. Anglers should pack a pair of polarized sunglasses, helpful on the glaring flats for spotting those wily bonefish.

And if you forget something? Don't worry. Grand Cayman has everything you'll need – clothing, medicines, watersports gear, camera equipment, you name it – albeit at prices somewhat higher than you might find at home.

❖ **TIP**

If you'll be making Little Cayman or Cayman Brac your home base, we recommend double-checking your packing list. Remember, these are remote islands with few stores. You'll find the basics but the selection will be slim.

Information Sources

For general information and brochures, call the **Cayman Islands Dept. of Tourism**, ☎ 800/346-3313.

On the Internet

The Cayman Islands Department of Tourism has an excellent Website: **www.cayman islands.ky**. Here you'll find the latest Cayman news and current weather conditions as well as tourism information including: hotels and condominiums; restaurants; transportation; attractions; fishing; scuba diving; snorkeling; group and meeting facilities; watersports; information on the Sister Islands; visitor services; links to other Cayman sites; an e-mail link to the DOT; a brochure request form.

Tourist Offices in the US

Before your trip, contact the tourism office nearest you for brochures and information.

Miami: 6100 Blue Lagoon Drive, Suite 150, Miami, FL 33126-2085, ☎ 305/266-2300.

New York: 420 Lexington Avenue, Suite 2733, New York, NY 10170; ☎ 212/682-5582.

Houston: Two Memorial City Plaza, 820 Gessner, Suite 170, Houston, TX 77024; ☎ 713/461-1317.

Los Angeles: 3440 Wilshire Boulevard, Suite 1202, Los Angeles, CA 90010; ☎ 213/738-1968

Chicago: 9525 W. Bryn Mawr Avenue, Suite 160, Rosemont, IL 60018; ☎ 708/678-6446.

Canada: 234 Eglinton Avenue East, Suite 306, Toronto, Ontario, Canada M4P 1K5; ☎ 416/485-1550.

United Kingdom: 6 Arlington Street, London, SW1A 1RE, England, United Kingdom; ☎ 0171/491-7771.

For more overseas offices, see page 24.

Help On-Island

When on Grand Cayman, visit the **Cayman Islands Department of Tourism** office at Elgin Avenue, Cricket Square in George Town or call ☎ 345/949-0623, fax 345/949-4053. You'll also find information booths with maps and brochures at the **Owen Roberts International Airport** and the **North Terminal** cruise ship dock.

❖ TIP

Be sure to stop by the tourist office to pick up 2-for-1 dinner coupons and shopping discounts.

Upon Arrival

Money Matters $

Cash

The **Cayman Islands dollar** is legal tender. The dollar is exchanged at a rate fixed to the US dollar (CI $1 equals US $1.25). The Cayman Islands dollar is issued in units of $100, $50, $25, $10, $5 and $1 with coins of 25 cents, 10, 5 and one cent.

★ DID YOU KNOW?

There's no need to exchange your money upon arrival – US dollars are readily accepted on the Cayman Islands. You may receive change back in Caymanian currency.

Tips of 10-15% are the standard. Gratuities are often added to restaurant bills; check first.

Credit Cards

Visa, Mastercard, American Express, Diners Club, and Access are commonly accepted; Discover is accepted at some establishments.

Telephones, Faxes & Internet Connections

The Cayman Islands have excellent telecommunications service thanks to Cable & Wireless (Cayman Islands) Ltd. You'll find dependable, modern phone and Internet service on each of the islands.

Due to the influence of the banking industry, these islands once had the largest per capita number of telex machines in the world, so good telecommunications have long been a necessity. Today you can count on facsimile services at just about every accommodation in the islands.

The area code for the Cayman Islands is 345. AT&T, MCI Direct and US Sprint services are available for dialing from the islands to home. Access numbers are:

US Sprint	☎ 888/366-4663
MCI Direct	☎ 800/624-1000
AT&T USA Direct	☎ 800/872-2881

The cost for local calls within Grand Cayman is nine cents for the first three minutes, three cents for each additional minute. Calls within either Little Cayman or Cayman Brac are charged a flat fee of nine cents per minute. Calls between Grand Cayman and the Sister Islands are three cents per minute. Calls between Little Cayman and Cayman Brac are nine cents per minute.

Throughout the islands, you'll find many public phones. Some accept coins only; others accept phone cards only; some accept both. You can purchase phone cards in denominations of $10, $15 and $25 at the Cable and Wireless office on Anderson Square on Shedden Road in George Town, at the Cayman Brac office and at most service stations.

Internet Connections

You'll find good Web service. Connections can be made by dialing (locally) ☎ 345/976-4638; the cost is CI 12¢ per minute.

Time Zone

The Cayman Islands are in the Eastern Time Zone, five hours behind Greenwich Mean Time. The Cayman Islands do not observe Daylight Savings Time.

Electrical Current

Throughout the islands, the current is 120 volts at 60 cycles. US appliances will not need adapters. The standard US flat pin prongs are used.

Crime

W e're happy to say that the Cayman Islands enjoy a low crime rate. With the islands' excellent economic position, crime is rare. You can walk on public beaches or stroll along busy West Bay Street after an evening meal without worrying about being mugged.

But no destination is completely crime-free. Use the same common sense precautions you would exercise at home. Don't walk alone on the beach at night. Also, don't leave valuables on the beach while swimming. Invest in a water-proof pouch for keys and necessities and lock other items in your car or hotel room.

❋ TIP

Many of the Cayman Islands' rental vehicles are open-air jeeps; to guard against theft leave your possessions in your hotel room when you venture out.

Drugs

Be warned that the islands have strict anti-drug laws. Marijuana is an illegal substance and possession can result not only in large fines but also in a prison term. There is no hassling by beach vendors and we have never been bothered by a drug salesman, which can be a problem on many other islands.

Media

Television

At most hotels and condominiums, you'll find as many television channels as you would at home, thanks to satellite broadcasts. The islands also have three local television stations: **CITN** (channel 27), **CTS** (channel 24) and **CCT**, Cayman Christian Television (channel 21).

Radio

Four local radio stations can be enjoyed as you drive around the islands. **Radio Cayman**, owned by the government, is broadcast on all the islands. **Z-99** broadcasts on Grand Cayman and **ICCI-FM**, at the International College of the Cayman Islands, also serves the largest island. Christian radio is heard on **Heaven 97**.

Newspapers

International newspaper prices are high.

Grand Cayman has a daily paper, the *Caymanian Compass*. You'll also be able to pick up US newspapers such as the *New York Times, USA Today*, and *The Wall Street Journal* at newsstands and hotel shops.

> ### ❊ TIP
>
> Avoid the high cost of imported newspapers by asking your hotel or condominium if they subscribe to *The New York Times* fax service, a digest of the day's news.

Culture & Customs

What to Expect

The Cayman Islands has a very American atmosphere. You'll feel at home instantly, but you should recognize that there are some subtle cultural differences.

With its long history of British rule, there is a slightly more formal atmosphere in personal relations – people are often introduced as Mr. or

Ms. Also, as in most of the Caribbean, it's traditional to greet others with "Good morning" or "Good afternoon" and a smile rather than just launching into your question or request.

Language

English is the primary language in the Cayman Islands, and it is spoken with a unique lilt, one a little different from accents in other areas of the Caribbean. It's a reminder of the islands' earliest ancestors with Welsh, Scottish, and English heritage. You'll often hear Jamaican patois as well.

★ DID YOU KNOW?

Because English is the official language, you will quickly notice that it follows British, not American, spellings such as colour, travellers, and centre.

Holidays

During public holidays, expect all government offices and most retail establishments to close.

OFFICIAL GOVERNMENT HOLIDAYS	
Month	Date/Holiday
January	1st - New Year's Day
February	Ash Wednesday
March, April	Good Friday, Easter Monday
May	19th - Discovery Day
June	16th - Queen's Birthday
July	Constitution Day (1st Monday)
November	10th - Remembrance Day
December	25th - Christmas Day 26th - Boxing Day

Festivals

The above may represent all the official government holidays, but by no means is that the end of the partying on these islands. You'll find special events throughout the year.

❈ Annual Mardi Gras Parade

Little Cayman. Mid-February.

❈ Annual St. Patrick's Day Jog

March 17. Grand Cayman.

❊ **Caylest**

This is the National Culture and Arts Festival. April (the whole month!). Grand Cayman.

❊ **Batabano Carnival and Parade**

Live music and Caymanian food. Bring your costume! Late April. Grand Cayman.

❊ **Cayman Islands International Fishing Tournament**

Late April, early May. Grand Cayman.

❊ **Cayman Brac Caylest**

April.

❊ **Cayman Islands International Aviation Week**

Early June. Grand Cayman.

❊ **Taste of Cayman**

Early July. Grand Cayman.

❊ **Pirates Week**

Be sure to bring your pirate's costume for this blowout! Late October, Grand Cayman.

For more details on Pirates Week, contact the festival office at ☎ 345/949-5078 or 949-5859.

❊ **Johnnie Walker Golf Tournament**

October. Grand Cayman.

For information on Cayman festivals, call the Cayman Islands Department of Tourism at ☎ 800/346-3313.

Weddings

Getting married in the islands is a simple affair. Non-residents need a special license granted by the Governor and once that license is obtained there is no residency period. A marriage license costs CI $150, plus a stamp duty.

Required Marriage Documents

* Original or certified birth certificate or passport.
* Cayman Islands international embarkation card.
* Certified or original copies of divorce decree (if applicable).
* Certified or original death certificate (if applicable).
* Marriage license.

Couples should write for a copy of the free brochure "Getting Married in the Cayman Islands" from Government Information Services, Broadcasting House, Grand Cayman (☎ 345/949-8092, fax 345/949-5936).

Grand Cayman

Grand Cayman is, as the name suggests, the largest of the three Cayman Islands. This is true not only in size, but in the number of attractions it offers. The 76-square-mile island, approximately 22 miles long and eight miles at its widest point, is chock-full of luxurious hotels and condominiums, beach bars, fine restaurants, duty-free shops, and plenty of soft adventure ranging from sunset cruises to scuba diving with stingrays.

Offshore Banking

One of the first things you'll notice about Grand Cayman is its affluence. Don't look for beach vendors or hair braiders along Seven Mile Beach – they're prohibited in this nation. The Cayman Islands enjoy one of the highest standards of living in the hemisphere, so expect to see nice cars, well-maintained streets, and signs of prosperity.

Much of that affluence comes from its successful tourism industry, 70% of its national product. Last year over $250 million was added to local coffers through tourism. The popularity of the islands continues to rise, and the most recent figures showed 1,144,313 annual visitors. Just over 373,000 arrive by air and over

771,000 by cruise ship. Those figures are up by 100,000 visitors from the previous year.

Most visitors arrive from the States, although which part of the US varies by time of year. During the winter season, many come from the East and Midwest; in hot summer months a great number of Texans and Southerners make their way to these islands, which are cooler than their own home states during that time.

Offshore financial services play an integral role in the islands' success as well. Grand Cayman has over 500 licensed banks (including 47 of the 50 largest banks worldwide). Banking secrecy laws passed in 1966 laid the groundwork for this profitable industry that today ranks the small island as the fifth largest financial center in the world, surpassed only by London, Tokyo, New York, and Hong Kong.

Offshore insurance companies are also a growing business. Nearly 400 offshore insurance or captive insurance companies make their base here. (Captive insurance is a term used for insurance companies set up by a company or a trade association to serve its members or employees.) Thanks to Cayman Islands' generous tax-free status, many other companies choose to incorporate in the islands; currently almost 30,000 companies are registered here.

A Cayman Bank Account

Just what is a Cayman bank account? Some are, as might be expected, multi-million dollar accounts, while others are much smaller in scale. Both take advantage of the tax-free status and confidentiality laws. These laws protect all reputable transactions as a means for earning tax-free interest. You can open an account once the Caymanian bank receives a reference from your home banker, then you can deposit funds (in US dollars, if you like). Unlike some countries, there is no exchange control and your money can be moved in and out of the country freely and privately.

The banks normally don't accept huge amounts of cash.

Because of the banking and offshore insurance industries, you'll notice that Grand Cayman has a different atmosphere than many other Caribbean islands. Here you'll find many returning guests, folks who are required by corporate charter to meet several times a year on the island (what a tough break!). You'll also meet many Americans who own property on Grand Cayman and live part of the year on the sunny isle. You'll also see many people combining a business trip with a few days of R&R.

But don't think that this is a suit-and-tie suit island; Grand Cayman is as laid-back as any other fun-in-the-sun site.

So where to start? If you'll be arriving by air or cruise ship, you'll start off in George Town, the capital of the island and the center of its business, transportation and shopping industry. From George Town, most visitors head to Seven Mile Beach, the center of the tourism industry, filled with luxury hotels, condominiums, restaurants, dive operators, and more. For more on the layout of George Town, Seven Mile Beach, and other areas of the island, see the *Orientation* section (page 62).

Getting There

*L*ucky travelers arrive on Grand Cayman by day, which affords them the perfect chance to see the varying colors of the waters that surround the small island, an indication of the shallows and depths that tempt scuba divers and snorkelers. From the air you'll also see the **North Sound**, home of **Stingray City**, and the white sands of **Seven Mile Beach**. Take a deep breath – you're almost there.

Located near George Town, **Owen Roberts International Airport** is a modern facility that has recently enlarged its baggage claim and immigration area.

❊ **TIP**

Despite improvements, we still suggest scooting off the plane as fast as you can because lines at Immigration do back up.

Once you're through immigration and customs, you'll find a tourist board office near baggage claim. Here you can load up on brochures and maps plus two-for-one coupons for some of the restaurants.

❄ **TIP**

At the tourist desk be sure to pick up a copy of the free *Key* or *Destination Cayman* magazines for information on shopping, dining, and nightly entertainment. *What to Do Cayman* and *What's Hot! in Cayman* also offer information on places of interest to visitors. And in case you didn't fly in on Cayman Airways or if you left your in-flight magazine, you can pick up a copy of their magazine, *Horizons*.

Step outside the airport to meet your ride or get a taxi to your hotel. Many car rental agencies are located across the street.

Getting To Your Hotel

Travelers bound for Seven Mile Beach will find that they're just minutes from their hotel after arriving at the airport. And if you're staying on the East End of the island, you'll be in for a quiet, leisurely drive (the traffic dies out once you leave George Town) and the chance to unwind a little before hitting the beach.

The hotels of Seven Mile Beach are a 10-minute drive from the airport. Taxi fare runs about US $4 per person, each way.

Getting Around

Car & Jeep Rentals

The low crime rate and excellent road system of the Cayman Islands encourage visitors to get out and explore. On each of the three Cayman Islands, attractions, beaches, small restaurants, and interesting sites are scattered, tempting vacationers to travel the countryside. Although taxi service is widespread on Grand Cayman, the easiest and most economical way for independent travelers to see the island is by rental car.

Car rentals begin at about US $30 per day; expect to pay US $43 per day for a 4x4 vehicle. Along with the rental fee, drivers will need to purchase a temporary driver's license. Licenses can be obtained by presenting a valid driver's license to the rental agency and paying the US $7.50 fee. A major credit card or cash deposit is also required. Renters must be age 21 or over; some agencies require renters to be 25 years of age.

The selection varies with location, but the greatest choice of rental cars is found on Grand Cayman. Here, 4x4 vehicles are commonplace and many travelers enjoy driving around the island in the open-air vehicles. Air-conditioned sedans and are also commonplace and often a better choice for families and those who want to secure their valuables while at the beach or in town. Most agencies feature American and Japanese models. Some offer unlimited mileage, free pick-up and drop-off, and free airport transfers.

Infant seats are available at some agencies, including Ace Hertz Rent-a-Car.

> ❋ **TIP**
>
> Many agencies such as Conmac, Thrifty, Brac Hertz, Four D's, and others offer the seventh day free.

On Grand Cayman, rental agencies are found at the airport, just across the street from the terminal building. Many rental agencies are also located in George Town and adjacent to major hotels along Seven Mile Beach.

Car Rental Agencies

Ace Hertz Rent-A-Car, ☎ 345/949-2280, fax 345/949-0572. Offers unlimited mileage; baby seats available. Features sedans, 4x4s. Located at Marriott.

Andy's Rent-a-Car, Ltd., ☎ 345/949-8111, fax 345/949-8385. Locations at the airport and along Seven Mile Beach opposite the Marriott. Features American cars.

Avis Cico, ☎ 345/949-2468, fax 345/949-7127. Located at the airport. Offers sedans, 4x4 soft tops. Also at Hyatt Regency Grand Cayman and Westin Casuarina hotels.

Budget Rent-A-Car, ☎ 345/949-5605, fax 345/949-2224. Offers sedans and vans.

Cayman Auto Rentals, ☎ 345/949-6408, fax 345/949-6500. Features 4x4s, sedans. Located in George Town.

Coconut Car Rentals, ☎ 345/949-4037, fax 345/949-7786. Features sedans, 4x4s; offers unlimited mileage.

Conmac Car Rental Transportation Company, ☎ 345/949-6955, fax 345/949-6955. Features sedans and 4x4s; seventh day free.

Dollar Rent-A-Car, ☎ 345/949-4790, fax 345/949-8484. Features sedans, jeeps, 4x4s; free pick-up and drop-off.

Economy Car Rental, ☎ 345/949-9550, fax 345/949-1003. Features jeeps, 4x4s, sedans; offers unlimited mileage, free pick-up and drop-off.

E. Scott Rent-A-Car, ☎ 345/949-8867, fax 345/949-8185. Features sedans, 4x4s, vans; offers unlimited mileage, free pick-up and drop-off.

Island Paradise Rent-A-Car, ☎ 345/949-5831, fax 345/949-1240. Features sedans, 4x4s; seventh day free.

Just Jeep Rentals, ☎ 345/949-7263, fax 345/949-0216, Website cayman.com/ky/com/jeep/index.htm. Offers 4x4s; deposit required. Free pick-up and drop-off along Seven Mile Beach.

Marshall's Rent-A-Car, ☎ 345/949-2127, fax 345/949-6435. Features sedans, luxury vans. Deposit required for cash rentals. Free airport drop-off. Located at Turtle Beach Villas.

Ole Jud's Rent-A-Car, ☎ 345/949-9333, fax 345/949-1431. Features sedans; offers unlimited miles and free airport drop-off.

Soto's 4 x4 Ltd., ☎ 345/949-2424, fax 345/949-2425; Website www.sotos4x4.ky. Offers 4x4s; offices at airport and Seven Mile Beach.

Thrifty Car Rental, ☎ 345/949-6640, fax 345/949-6354. Offers sports utility vehicles. Seventh day free; deposit required for cash rentals. All offer air-conditioning and unlimited mileage.

Scooters

If you want to buzz around the island on a scooter, **Cayman Cycle** has rentals at Treasure Island Resort (☎ 345/949-8711), the Hyatt Regency Grand Cayman (☎ 345/949-1234, ext. 3050), and Coconut Place (☎ 345/945-4021). Soto Sooters and Car Rentals (☎ 345/945-4652) at The Strand on West Bay Road, also offers rentals. Scooter rental averages $25 per day. A permit is required to drive a scooter and riding experience is necessary.

Bicycles

With its relatively flat grade, the Cayman Islands are a good destination for bicyclists. On Grand Cayman, however, note that along West Bay Road traffic can be extremely heavy during morning and evening rush hours. Prices vary, but average about $12 per day for a 10-speed bike and $14 for a mountain bike.

Bicycle Rental Agencies

Cayman Cycle Rentals at Treasure Island Resort (☎ 345/949-8711); Hyatt Regency Grand Cayman (☎ 345/949-1234, ext. 3050); and Coconut Place (☎ 345/945-4021).

Soto Sooters and Car Rentals (☎ 345/945-4652) at The Strand on West Bay Road.

Driving Tips

In true British tradition, traffic travels on the **left side** of the road. This can be confusing on your first day behind the wheel so start off a little slower than usual. Most cars are right-hand drive so that will also necessitate a few adjustments (on our first excursion we turned on the windshield wipers every time we tried to give a turn signal!).

In George Town, keep an eye out for **one-way streets** as well as **pedestrians**. Remember, many pedestrians, like you, are accustomed to cars being on the right side of the road and may step out at the wrong time.

Watch for yellow lines in the road. These indicate **no parking** areas.

Be sure to **stop behind any bus**; doors open out in the center of the road.

Watch for **speed limits** and note that **driving under the influence** is a serious offense in the Cayman Islands.

The toughest driving is along Seven Mile Beach as it makes its way into George Town. This island has a real **rush hour** both mornings and evenings, so budget a little (make that a lot) of extra time during those peak periods. During the evening hours, drive especially carefully along this stretch as well. It is packed with pedestrians strolling from hotels to restaurants, as well as vacationers out and about in cars.

Remember to look RIGHT when crossing the street!

Taxis

Taxi rates are based on a maximum of three riders. The minimum fee is CI $4 for the first mile, CI $1.75 for each additional mile. Waiting time is charged at CI 75¢ per minute.

Taxis can be found at most of the major hotels, down alongside the cruise terminal in George Town. They congregate beneath the shade trees, waiting for fares.

Bus Service

Grand Cayman recently launched its first public transportation service, a response to the increasing traffic found along Seven Mile Beach. Today a new bus terminal on Edward Street (near the Public Library) in downtown George Town serves as the hub for 38 minibuses. Fares range from CI $1.50 to CI $2.

Eight routes serve the island and include service to West Bay (the most frequent service, running every 15 minutes), Bodden Town, East End and North Side (once an hour). A bus also serves stops within George Town.

Look for blue license plates on these buses. For questions and schedules, ☎ 345/945-5100.

Exploring the Island

Island Tours

Experienced tour operators offer an in-depth look at the islands. Guides can provide a general overview as well as specialized tours focus-

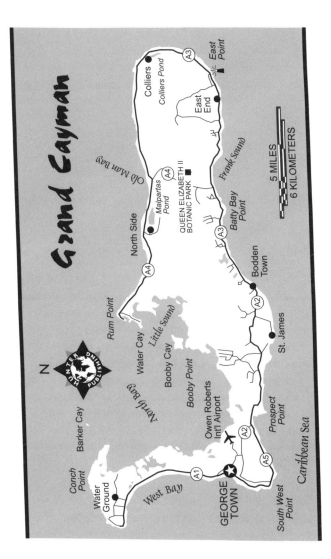

Grand Cayman

ing on eco-tourism, plants, history, birding, and shopping.

General island tours are offered by several companies. "Tours are personalized to give the visitor opportunity to expand his or her knowledge of the Cayman Islands and its people," says Burton Ebanks, owner of AA Transportation Services on Grand Cayman.

Vacationers can stop to mail postcards and have them postmarked from Hell.

Overviews of the island range from 2½ hours to all day. Typical tours include a drive-through look at the capital city of **George Town**, a photo stop at the **Conch Shell House** (a private residence made of conch shells), a cruise along **Seven Mile Beach**, a tour of the **Cayman Turtle Farm** (the world's only such operation), and a visit to the community of **Hell**.

Full-day tours include the same stops as a brief tour but also take a look at the less-visited east side of the island. Tours often drive through **Bodden Town**, visit the **Pirate's Caves**, stop for photos of the **Blow Holes**, and swing around to **Rum Point**, a popular watersports area overlooking the entrance to the North Sound.

"The attractions of the Cayman Islands are obvious and easy to find," points out Lisette Usborne, operations manager for Tropicana Tours Ltd. Nonetheless, guided tours still represent a valuable service even for those who might have a rental car during their stay. "Our tours encompass interesting details that the

George Town

This is the hub of the island. To really know the island you've got to tear yourself away from the white sands of Seven Mile Beach (at least for a little while) and explore this community. As home to over half the 30,000 residents of Grand Cayman and the base for most of the business and government activity, this is the capital of the Cayman Islands. Don't look for a bustling city, however; George Town is still very much an island community where you'll feel at home strolling the streets, eating at a seaside diner, and enjoying watersports just as you would in the resort areas of Seven Mile Beach.

George Town, located on the island's southwest corner, faces west and overlooks Hog Sty Bay and the George Town Harbour, a busy port where on any given day you'll probably find cruise ships as well as working vessels.

Much of the activity in George Town takes place along **North and South Church Streets**, which run north-south parallel to the shoreline. These roads face out to the harbor and are lined with duty-free shops, restaurants, and tourist-oriented businesses. The traffic light where South Church Street forks right onto Shedden Road or continues onto North Church Street (an intersection located by the cruise terminal) is the heart of town.

At this point, part of North Church St. is also called Harbour Drive. It's less complicated than it sounds – remember, this is still a small town.

Just north of the cruise terminal, you'll see the intersection of Harbour Drive and Cardinal

Avenue. **Cardinal Avenue** is the home of many duty-free shops.

> **★ DID YOU KNOW?**
>
> The intersection of Harbour Drive and Cardinal Avenue was featured in *The Firm*. Avery, Gene Hackman's character, makes a call from a phone booth as Tom Cruise looks out and sees an Abanks Dive Lodge advertisement.

Just south of the intersection with Cardinal Avenue lies the Shedden Road. Shedden Road heads east and soon becomes **Crewe Road**, which intersects with Owen Roberts Drive, the road to the airport. If you don't take the Owen Roberts Drive fork but veer right, you can stay on Crewe Road and head to the eastern part of the island.

East of the shoreline, government buildings and banking centers carry on the work of the Cayman Islands, helping the nation hold its spot as one of the major monetary centers of the world. Farther east is the **airport**, located on the edge of **North Sound**, the shallow body of water that divides George Town, Seven Mile Beach, and the West End from the less developed East End of the island.

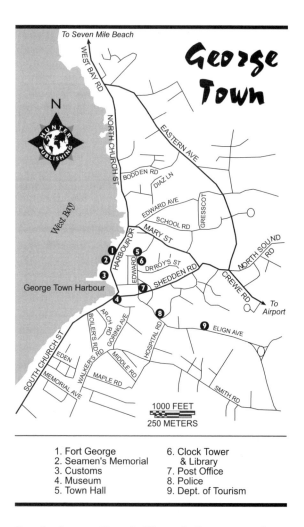

1. Fort George
2. Seamen's Memorial
3. Customs
4. Museum
5. Town Hall
6. Clock Tower & Library
7. Post Office
8. Police
9. Dept. of Tourism

South of town, **South Church Street** winds its way through elegant residential districts, lined with beautiful seaside homes and a few quiet businesses.

East End

East of George Town lies, predictably enough, the East End. One main road circles the entire East End, running east from George Town, tracing the shoreline as it snakes through small communities such as Bodden Town and Spotts. This road turns north at the end of the island and begins to trace the northern edge of the island, but you can take a shortcut halfway down the island on the **Frank Sound Road**, the route to the Queen Elizabeth II Botanic Gardens. When it comes out on the north side, the road travels west to **Rum Point**, a popular destination with vacationers who arrive by ferry from Seven Mile Beach and enjoy a day of fun in the sun. South of Rum Point, **Cayman Kai** is a quiet residential area filled with beautiful, expensive homes. Rum Point and Cayman Kai look west across the vast, shallow North Sound.

The point where North Sound meets the sea is the home of Stingray City, one of the top attractions on Grand Cayman.

Kai rhymes with lie.

Seven Mile Beach

There's something here for all skill levels: shallow dives and snorkel trips, cave and wreck dives. The waters teem with colorful tropical fish.

Across the North Sound lies a long stretch of land that is the main destination for most Cayman Islands vacationers. This is Seven Mile Beach, which sprawls north of George Town, sandwiched between the sea and the North Sound. This narrow strip of land may be small but it's not short on accommodations and restaurants; this is the heart of vacationland. Here dive shops, watersports operators, beach bars, sportswear shops, and fine restaurants stand shoulder to shoulder, separated by some fine-needled casuarina trees. They look out on a calm, baby-blue sea that covers some of the top scuba diving sites in the world.

North to south along Seven Mile Beach runs **West Bay Road**, the main thoroughfare and one that can sometimes get downright crowded. Along this road you'll find the lion's share of Cayman's tourism business.

Along Seven Mile Beach, Grand Cayman narrows to a skinny stretch about a mile wide, bordered by the beach on the west and North Sound to the east. On its eastern edges, the sea forms a rugged boundary, at some points etching into the land with salt creeks and harbors.

Much of these eastern reaches are covered by swampy vegetation.

The largest harbor along this stretch of North Sound is **Governors Harbour,** where Governors Creek offers a maze of natural and man-made canals. Today it's lined with luxury lots and lavish homes as well as the Cayman Islands Yacht Club.

West Bay

Finally, Seven Mile Beach ends in West Bay, the clump of land on the westernmost side of North Sound. This area is the home of the **Cayman Turtle Farm**, one of the most popular attractions with cruise tour operators and a great spot for families.

Traveling north from Seven Mile Beach along **West Bay Road**, the name of the road changes to **North West Point Road** and follows the coastline, becoming more and more residential. At the Cayman Turtle Farm, a less traveled road traces the far northern edge of this region, continually switching names along the route: Boatswains Bay Road, King Road, Birch Tree Hill Road, Conch Point Road, Palmetto Point Road. Traveling west, houses become fewer and fewer and the area gives way to a swampy habitat.

Wattle & Daub Houses

West Bay is home to many traditional Caymanian houses built of wattle and daub. The technique used ironwood posts to support walls woven with cabbagewood. The wood was then plastered over with daub, a mortar that includes burned coral. Making the daub was often a neighborhood activity since it was so labor intensive. This style was sturdy and could withstand the hurricanes and tropical storms as well as rain and sun. This technique is no longer used.

Or you can turn away from the coast and head to the inland area of West Bay to a community called **Hell**, a popular stop on island tours. Follow Hell Road East onto Reverend Blackman Road and then Batabano Road to travel to North Sound and to the fishing community of **Batabano**. This is home of **Morgans Harbour**, starting point for many deep-sea fishing

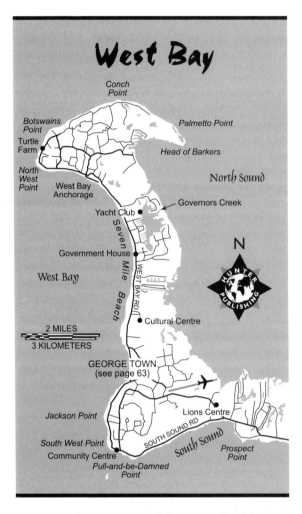

West Bay

Conch Point

Botswains Point

Palmetto Point

Turtle Farm

Head of Barkers

North West Point

North Sound

West Bay Anchorage

Governors Creek

Yacht Club

Government House

Seven Mile Beach

WEST BAY RD

N

West Bay

HUNTER PUBLISHING

2 MILES
3 KILOMETERS

Cultural Centre

GEORGE TOWN
(see page 63)

Jackson Point

Lions Centre

South West Point

SOUTH SOUND RD

South Sound

Community Centre

Prospect Point

Pull-and-be-Damned Point

cruises and some tours of Stingray City. It's not as glitzy as Seven Mile Beach, but offers an interesting look at a working side of Grand Cayman.

Best Places to Stay

The Cayman Islands offers over 2,300 hotel rooms and more than 2,100 condominium and villa units, most found on Grand Cayman. While some of these cater to a dive crowd seeking low-cost, no-frills accommodations, most properties on Grand Cayman are for a medium to upscale market.

Room prices vary greatly with type of accommodation, location, and time of year. High season (mid-December through mid-April) brings prices about 40% higher than in summer months.

A 10% government tax is charged on all accommodations. Most hotels add gratuities ranging from 6-10% to this amount.

Most accommodations are found along Seven Mile Beach. These are divided into properties on the west side or beach side of the road and those on the east, which don't have direct access to the beach.

Just a reminder of the price scale we're using:

Alive Price Scale - Accommodations

Deluxe . . . . $300+

Expensive . . . . $200-$300

Moderate . . . . $100-$200

Inexpensive . . . . Under $100

Resorts & Hotels

BEACH CLUB COLONY
West Bay Road
Grand Cayman
☎ 345/949-8100, fax 345/945-5167
Reservations: ☎ 800/482-DIVE
Moderate

As its name suggests, this all-inclusive resort is tucked right on the beachfront. It offers 41 guest rooms. All come with telephones, air-conditioning and television. There are laundry facilities, a pool, restaurant and bar, dive shop, snorkeling, sailing, windsurfing, fishing, tennis, and more.

Children under age six stay free with parents.

CARIBBEAN CLUB
Seven Mile Beach
Grand Cayman
☎ 345/945-4099, fax 345/945-4443
www.caribclub.com
Expensive

The Caribbean Club offers 18 one- and two-bedroom pastel pink villas and the opportunity for relaxation. Six of the villas are situated on the beachfront; others have a garden view. All rooms include a full kitchen, air-conditioning, ceiling fan, TV, phone, dining room, and furnished patio.

GRAND CAYMAN MARRIOTT BEACH RESORT

Seven Mile Beach
Grand Cayman
☎ 345/949-0088, fax 345/949-0288
Reservations: ☎ 800/223-6388
Expensive

We love this property and have enjoyed visiting here many times, dating back to its days as a Radisson. Recently the property has undergone an extensive renovation and it's better than ever.

Located two miles from George Town and about four miles from the airport, this convenient property is set on a beautiful stretch of Seven Mile Beach. Swimmers and snorkelers can enjoy calm waters and a small coral reef just offshore or learn scuba diving. Dive trips may be booked through the on-site shop.

The Marriott is known for its guest rooms, the largest on the island. All have been recently renovated; 80% of the rooms feature king-sized beds. Oceanfront rooms include private balconies with good beach views and are worth the somewhat long walk to the elevators in this 315-room hotel. Facilities include casual and fine dining, pool and hot tub, dive shop, wave runners, windsurfing, shopping arcade, and full-service spa.

HYATT REGENCY GRAND CAYMAN
Seven Mile Beach
Grand Cayman
☎ 345/949-1234, fax 345/949-8528
Reservations: ☎ 800/233-1234
Expensive

If you're looking for either a beach resort with a full range of amenities or a business hotel with plenty of free time options, this place fits the bill. This longtime favorite recently underwent an expansion to offer rooms directly on Seven Mile Beach and to increase its watersports and recreational facilities.

The Hyatt has the atmosphere of a country club with the amenities of an island resort. The hotel's amenities flow out from a great main house. The grounds are dotted with royal palms and ponds are filled with colorful koi. There's a freeform swimming pool, complete with bridges and pool bar. Blocks of guest rooms circle this central area; Britannia Villas lie beyond, adjacent to the golf course. Shuttle service is available from the main house to the villas and spa.

★ DID YOU KNOW?
The Aquas Pool Bar in the original section of the resort was featured in *The Firm*. Remember when Jeanne Tripplehorn's character shows up on the island to surprise Avery (Gene Hackman)? She meets him in this bar.

Families make up a growing portion of the hotel's business, thanks to the Camp Hyatt program which features villa accommodations with kitchen facilities and the many recreational options.

Golfers appreciate the Britannia golf course. Many guest rooms overlook the course, designed by Jack Nicklaus, or the private marina. Standard rooms, each carpeted and featuring a soft Caribbean color scheme, include a mini-bar, satellite color television, coffee makers with complimentary coffee, electronic key card system, direct dial telephones with voice mail, in-room safe, ironing board, and hairdryer. Along with standard rooms, the property includes 50 one-, two-, three-, and four-bedroom villas and 10 bi-level suites. The Britannia Villas are especially popular with families and include all the hotel amenities except turndown service. A separate Regency Club offers 44 rooms that include complimentary continental breakfast, evening cocktails and hors d'oeuvres, concierge service, upgraded amenities and linens, and use of the Regency Club lounge.

A recent $15 million addition features 53 beachfront suites on Seven Mile Beach. These suites have a separate living room that includes a dining area, wet bar, work station with two phone lines, and upgraded amenities. All suites have sea views, and these rooms are served by a dedicated concierge. The complex is highlighted by a new landscaped pool complex with bronze sea turtle sculptures, waterfalls, and three freshwater pools with mosaic tile designs of stingrays and other marine life.

Access from the existing resort to the new addition is via a crosswalk with elevator access over West Bay Road.

Red Sail Sports has opened a 2,000-square-foot state-of-the-art diving center as part of the beach addition. The center serves as Red Sail's main on-island training facility with dedicated classroom space, an on-site eight-foot training pool and locker room as well as a retail shop that includes photo/video editing and developing facilities. Red Sail offers a range of watersports, including catamaran cruises on two 65-foot vessels for dinner sails, cocktail cruises, and luncheon snorkel excursions to Stingray City. Dive boats offer one- and two-tank trips as well as night dives. Sea kayaking, waverunners, waterskiing, parasailing, and underwater photography are also available as well as deep-sea, bone, and reef fishing.

The Hyatt runs a ferry to Rum Point, on the tip of the East End. After $5 million in renovations, Rum Point is now filled with beachside fun, including a full-service dinner restaurant, casual lunch eatery and bar, decks and walkways, plenty of comfy hammocks and picnic tables, a gift shop, and more.

The resort opened Grand Cayman's first full-service spa with complete facilities.

For an additional fee, children aged three-12 can take part in the Camp Hyatt Grand Cayman program, available daily during the summer months, Easter, Thanksgiving, and Christmas holidays and weekends year-round.

INDIES SUITES
Seven Mile Beach
Grand Cayman
☎ 345/945-5025, fax 345/945-5024
Reservations: ☎ 800/954-3130
Moderate to expensive

Although it doesn't have a beachfront location, Indies Suites is a good choice if you're looking for suite accommodations. All rooms include either a king-size or two double beds and a full-size kitchen equipped for four. All rooms also include satellite TV, telephone, storage locker for dive gear, and convertible sofa bed. The family-operated all-suites hotel includes a dive shop and a free resort course for an introduction to scuba diving. There's also a pool, hot tub, cabana bar, boutique, mini-mart, and complimentary continental breakfast daily.

MORRITT'S TORTUGA CLUB
East End
Grand Cayman
☎ 345/947-7449, fax 345/947-7669
Reservations: ☎ 800/447-0309
Moderate

A favorite with divers and windsurfers, this East End resort is located right on the beach. Amenities include air-conditioning, ceiling fans, phones, TV, kitchenettes, pool, Jacuzzi, restaurant, bar, dive shop, scuba trips, snorkeling, sailing, windsurfing, fishing, and more.

SLEEP INN
Seven Mile Beach
☎ 345/949-9111, fax 345/949-6699
Reservations: ☎ 800/SLEEP INN
Inexpensive

If you're in search of a centrally located place to lay your head after a day of fun in the sun, the Sleep Inn is a good choice. This chain motel is just outside of George Town along the Seven Mile Beach stretch (the hotel itself is not on the beach). Rooms include air-conditioning, telephones; the property has a pool and whirlpool, poolside bar and grill, dive shop, and watersports center.

SPANISH BAY REEF
West Bay
☎ 345/949-3765, fax 345/949-1842
Reservations: ☎ 800/482-DIVE
Expensive

Located on the far northwest end of West Bay, Spanish Bay Reef is a good all-inclusive choice. Tucked on a sandy stretch of beach shaded by tall palms and willowy casuarina trees, the resort is casual and fun. The sea here is somewhat choppy, although a barrier creates a swimming area. This resort is a favorite with divers. Dive sites include No Name Wall, Chinese Wall, Lemon Drop-Off, Grand Canyon, The Pinnacles, and more, each offering divers a peek at an undersea world filled with marine life, fascinating formations, and beautiful corals.

All rooms offer air-conditioning and private balcony or patio and satellite TV. Amenities include The Spanish Main Restaurant and Calico Jack's Poolside Bar as well as a private beach, freshwater pool, Jacuzzi, and dock.

The all-inclusive meals and beverages (well drinks only, no wine or champagne), use of sightseeing cars on a shared basis, bicycle, introductory scuba and snorkeling lessons, unlimited scuba diving from shore for certified divers (including tanks and weight belt), boat dive (usually a two-tank dive), airport transfers, and all taxes and gratuities.

WESTIN CASUARINA RESORT
Seven Mile Beach
☎ 345/945-3800, fax 345/949-5825
Reservations: ☎ 800/228-3000
Deluxe

We visited this property when construction was still underway and every time we return we are reminded how much we love the finished product. The newest hotel in Grand Cayman is built on a strip of beach bordered by willowy casuarina trees. There are 340 guest rooms, most with breathtaking views of the sea from step-out balconies. The hotel has the feel of a conference property, with a slightly dress-up atmosphere in the main lobby.

Facilities include beachfront, casual and fine dining restaurants, pools, whirlpools, tennis, fitness facilities, beauty salons, masseuse and masseur.

Condominiums

When it comes to condominiums, there's one word to describe the current state of business: booming. New projects are dotting the islands. Travelers can now choose from a great number of condominiums, villas, and guest houses, whether they're headed to the islands for diving, honeymooning, or just some R&R.

Amenities at condominiums vary with price. You can expect microwaves, dishwasher, washer/dryer, cable TV, and central air at most properties. Others will include private swimming pools, hot tubs, and more. A few properties offer honeymoon, golf, dive, and escape packages.

The most recent statistics show that Grand Cayman offers 2,170 condominium rooms & 2,331 hotel rooms.

In the last few years, there has been a real trend toward super-luxurious condominiums on this island. "More and more private houses and exclusive (super deluxe) condos are being built," notes Penny Cumber, managing director for Cayman Villas. "Both houses and condos are becoming more deluxe, and many have a private pool, some with Jacuzzi and gym."

THE ANCHORAGE
Seven Mile Beach
☎ 345/945-4088, fax 345/945-5001
Expensive

This group of 15 villas has two bedrooms per unit and offers televisions, VCRs, kitchen, laundry facilities, maid service, barbecue grills, pool, a dive shop, and tennis.

AQUA BAY CLUB

☎ 345/945-4728, fax 345/945-5681
Reservations: ☎ 800/825-8703
www.grand-bay.com
Deluxe

This 21-unit condominium resort on Seven Mile Beach recently underwent an extensive renovation. "A total remodeling within the past year including new landscaping as well as a new roof brought our property well above the standard," points out Walter Puk, director of marketing. Honeymooners, divers, golfers, families and couples are target markets for this property with one- and two-bedroom oceanfront units. Each unit has a view of the sea and all are fully equipped. Guest facilities include a freshwater pool, tennis, and Jacuzzi.

Unlike most condominium properties on Grand Cayman, Aqua Bay Club (formerly Grand Bay Club) offers guests the option of packages. "At present it is the only property offering honeymoon, golf, dive and escape packages. Future plans include a dine around package as well as an air-inclusive package," notes Walter Puk.

THE AVALON

Seven Mile Beach
☎ 345/945-4171, fax 345/945-4189
Deluxe

A 27-unit complex offering three-bedroom condos sleeping four to six guests. Located four miles from George Town, this deluxe property includes televisions, VCRs, kitchen and laundry facilities, maid service, handicapped-accessible rooms, barbecue grills, and more.

BEACHCOMBER CONDOMINIUMS
Seven Mile Beach
☎ 345/945-4470, fax 345/945-5019
www.ars1.com/beachcomber
Deluxe

Right on Seven Mile Beach, this property has 24 guest units. Rooms come with air-conditioning, telephone, television, VCR, kitchen, laundry service, maid service, and use of pool. There's great snorkeling right off the beach here.

CASA CARIBE
Seven Mile Beach
☎ 345/945-4287, fax 345/945-5151
Deluxe

This property has 24 units. It includes facilities such as tennis, snorkeling, pool, Jacuzzi, and more.

CAYMAN REEF RESORT
Seven Mile Beach
☎ 345/949-7819, fax 345/949-9751
Expensive to Deluxe

This 62-room condominium resort has a variety of guest facilities to keep you busy. There's night tennis, snorkeling, pool, barbecue, grills, babysitting, mail service. Many acitivities are offered.

CORAL SANDS RESORT
Seven Mile Beach
☎ 345/949-4400, fax 345/949-4005
Expensive

Each of the 12 guest rooms at the Coral Sands includes two bedrooms, a living and dining room, and a fully equipped kitchen. The property is just about a mile from the center of George Town.

THE CORALSTONE CLUB
Seven Mile Beach
☎ 345/945-5820, fax 345/945-5917
Deluxe

Thirty-seven guest rooms are available at this Seven Mile Beach property situated about six miles from George Town. Guests have use of tennis courts. Additional amenities include telephones, televisions, VCRs, maid service, and more.

DISCOVERY POINT CLUB
West Bay
☎ 345/945-4724, fax 345/945-5051
www.mjwebworks.com/discovery
Expensive

This beachside complex has 45 suites. The one- and two-bedroom apartments include air-conditioning, screened porches or balconies, telephone, and TV. Units have kitchens, but some gardenview hotel-type units are available without kitchens. Facilities include Jacuzzi, pool, and tennis.

GEORGE TOWN VILLAS
George Town
☎ 345/949-5172, fax 345/949-0256
Deluxe

This 54-unit complex is about 1½ miles from George Town. Guest activities include tennis and snorkeling.

THE GRANDVIEW
Seven Mile Beach
☎ 345/945-4511, fax 345/949-7515
Reservations: ☎ 800/872-7552
www.grandviewcondos.com
Deluxe

Sixty-nine guest units are available at this complex on Seven Mile Beach. Guest activities include tennis and scuba (there's a dive shop on property).

HARBOUR HEIGHTS
Seven Mile Beach
☎ 345/945-4295, fax 345/945-4522
Expensive to Deluxe

These condos have views of the ocean and each offers a full kitchen, living and dining area. Each of the 46 units includes two bedrooms. Guests enjoy a pool and snorkeling on site.

THE HERITAGE CLUB
Seven Mile Beach
☎ 345/945-4993, fax 345/945-5119
Deluxe

These 18 units offer two bedrooms as well as tennis and a swimming pool.

ISLAND PINE VILLAS
Seven Mile Beach
☎ 345/949-6586, fax 345/949-0428
Expensive

Forty units offer one or two bedrooms. Guests have use of tennis facilities and can snorkel right offshore.

THE ISLANDS CLUB
Seven Mile Beach
☎ 345/945-5211, fax 345/949-0680
www.cayman.com.ky/com/islclub
Deluxe

Guests select from 26 units; two or three bedrooms are available in each unit. Amenities include tennis courts and snorkel facilities.

LACOVIA CONDOMINIUMS
Seven Mile Beach
☎ 345/949-7599, fax 345/949-0172
Reservations: ☎ 800/445-8945
Deluxe

Lacovia offers 55 one- , two- , and three-bedroom units. Tennis facilities on site.

LONDON HOUSE
Seven Mile Beach
☎ 345/945-4069, fax 345/945-4087
Deluxe

Located on Seven Mile Beach, these oceanfront condos offer summer specials (such as stay for seven nights, pay for five). The 21 units have either two or three bedrooms. Guests can play tennis, snorkel or book fishing trips on site.

PAN CAYMAN HOUSE
Seven Mile Beach
☎ 345/945-4002, fax 345/945-4011
Reservations: ☎ 800/248-5115
Deluxe

These 10 units have either two or three bedrooms. Snorkeling is right offshore.

PLANTANA CONDOMINIUMS
Seven Mile Beach
☎ 345/945-4430, fax 345/945-5076
Expensive to Deluxe

This 49-unit complex offers elegant condominium accommodations just steps from the sandy
beach. Two- and four-guest units are available.
Each comes with air-conditioning as well as
ceiling fans, telephones, television, kitchens
and maid service. Laundry facilities are available.

PLANTATION VILLAGE
BEACH RESORT
Seven Mile Beach
☎ 345/949-4199, fax 345/949-0646
Reservations: ☎ 800/822-8903
Expensive to Deluxe

This complex boasts bright, sunny rooms right
on Seven Mile Beach. The 70 guests units feature air-conditioning, TV, VCR, maid service,
kitchen and more. Free use of kayaks, road
bikes, lighted tennis courts and other amenities.

SEVEN MILE BEACH RESORT & CLUB
Seven Mile Beach
☎ 345/949-0332, fax 345/949-0331
Deluxe

Located inland but with private beach facilities, this condominium property offers two-bedroom, two-bath units. Each has a private balcony, air-conditioning, telephone, cable TV, VCR, and a fully equipped kitchen. The complex includes a freshwater pool, Jacuzzi, lighted tennis court, outdoor grills, and children's play area.

Seven Mile Watersports arranges trips to Stingray City and has complete dive facilities, including resort and certification courses.

TREASURE ISLAND CONDOMINIUMS
Seven Mile Beach
☎ 515/435-2001, fax 515/435-2002
Reservations: ☎ 800/999-1338
Deluxe

This 280-room resort includes an offshore snorkel trail. Now starting to look a little tired around the edges, the hotel nonetheless has a pretty pool area with waterfall cascading down from the third floor restaurant.

Facilities include two freshwater pools, two whirlpools, tennis, dive operation, shopping, informal dining, bar, and lounge.

VILLAGE OF BRITANNIA
Seven Mile Beach
☎ 345/949-1234, fax 345/949-8032
Reservations: ☎ 800/233-1234
Deluxe

The Britannia Villas are especially popular with families and include all the hotel amenities except turndown service. These condominiums are part of the Hyatt resort (see above) and guests have full use of the facilities at the adjacent hotel. The villas are located along the Britannia golf course and are a short walking distance from the beach.

VILLAS OF THE GALLEON
Seven Mile Beach
☎ 345/945-4433, fax 345/945-4705
Deluxe

This is a popular 74-unit complex. It offers well-furnished units, and rooms include air-conditioning, telephone, TV, VCR, kitchen, laundry facilities, and maid service.

Villas

Villas appeal to many types of vacationers. Penny Cumber, managing director for Cayman Villas, says that the properties are especially favored by "honeymooners, who opt for the quiet private houses and condos or close to action, families with young children (especially houses/condos all one level and ground floor), families with older children (houses within walking distance of watersports), large family reunions or a large gathering of friends (seeking condos/houses close by), wedding parties and guests in nearby villas, and couples celebrating special occasions."

Properties are closely inspected and monitored to maintain high standards. "All our villas (houses and condos) are inspected by ourselves, as well as the Department of Tourism, and departments of fire and environment. They inspect furnishings, linens, flooring, woodwork, metal fixtures, landscaping, beach, quality of drinkable water, and check for fire extinguishers and detectors, etc. They (and we) are very tough! All villas are professionally sprayed by pest control specialists. All are in excellent shape and good quality," says Cumber

CAYMAN VILLAS

☎ 345/945-4144, fax 345/949-7471
Reservations: ☎ 800/235-5888
www.caymanvillas.com

Honeymooners & those celebrating a special occasion receive a complimentary bottle of champagne when they stay at any Cayman Villa property.

Cayman Villas manages numerous properties on Grand Cayman as well as on the Sister Islands. "More and more private houses and exclusive (very deluxe) condos are being built," notes Penny Cumber, managing director for Cayman Villas. "Both houses and condos are becoming more deluxe, many of which have a private pool, some with Jacuzzi and gym. Yes, there is a building boom and most especially on Grand Cayman and Little Cayman."

Aside from its most luxurious properties, Cayman Villas also offers properties for the average traveler. Over 100 properties, some starting at $99 a night, are represented. "Cayman Villas specializes in beachfront condos and private houses ranging from economy to deluxe, from studios to seven-bedroom properties. Most condos are on Seven Mile Beach. Most private houses are at Cayman Kai, but there are many other quiet beaches around Grand Cayman, Cayman Brac and Little Cayman, on which we also have villas. Guests can be on their own private beach and in the midst of all the action."

Here's a sampling of some of the island's many properties available through Cayman Villas:

THE GREAT HOUSE
Seven Mile Beach
Deluxe

These apartments, used by *The Firm* filmmakers, includes three bedrooms and a den that can become a private fourth bedroom. Rooms offer one king, one queen, two twin beds, and two day beds. The apartment has 3½ half baths, satellite TV and VCR, kitchen with microwave, dishwasher, icemaker, wine cellar, and washer/dryer, dining room, and beachfront balcony. Guests have use of a freshwater pool, tennis courts, and gym on premises. Just how much does all this super-luxury go for? At press time, the four-bedroom units rented for a minimum one-month stay for US $38,745 per month or you could reserve a three-bedroom unit for $1,475 per night in high season.

THE GREEN HOUSE
Spotts Beach
Deluxe

This new private home is situated on the beachfront about five minutes from the airport in George Town. The house includes four oceanview bedrooms (two masters each with king bed), four full ensuite bathrooms and a half guest bath, living and dining room with high ceilings, French doors to let in ocean breezes, kitchen with microwave, waste disposal, icemaker, and dishwasher, utility room, satellite TV and VCR, freshwater pool, and housekeeping services. Luxury comes at a hefty price for this property as well – current rates are $1,475 per night during peak months.

KAI SOUND
Cayman Kai
Moderate

This is a studio cottage on the beach at Cayman Kai. It has a kitchenette with microwave, washer/dryer, air-conditioning and use of two bicycles.

GEMENI
Cayman Kai
Expensive

This duplex has two one-bedroom, one-bath cottages. They include a living room, full kitchen and screened porch; you can step right onto the beach. Amenities include air-conditioning, telephone, TV and VCR, washer/dryer, icemaker and more.

HARBOUR VIEW
George Town
Inexpensive to moderate

This one-bedroom, one-bath apartment is within walking distance of George Town. It offers a living/dining room, full kitchen, and a patio with ocean view. There's daily maid service, TV, telephone and air-conditioning.

Small Hotels

SUNSET HOUSE RESORT
George Town
☎ 345/949-7111, fax 345/949-7101
Reservations: ☎ 800/854-4767
Moderate

Located just south of George Town, Sunset House is a favorite with divers. Just offshore lie both the reef and several shipwrecks, making this a virtual playground for those interested in underwater adventure.

There's nothing fancy about Sunset House – it's designed for those whose major portion of time is spent in the water, not necessarily on land. Guest rooms include standard accommodations overlooking the courtyard and deluxe rooms with ocean or garden views. Two suites are also available.

Divers and those who want to learn can utilize the full-service dive operation, which offers resort courses, certification courses, check-out dives, and advanced instruction. When you're suited up and ready to go, it's just a matter of stepping off the shore ladder and into the aqua-playground. For more distant dives, six custom boats take underwater enthusiasts on two-tank dives around the island while *Manta*, a catamaran, takes experienced divers on all-day, three-tank dives.

Facilities at this 59-room resort include a restaurant featuring local and continental cuisine, gift shop, oceanfront bar, freshwater swimming pool and hot tub, full-service dive shop, six dive boats, and the Sunset Underwater Photo Centre, which offers half-day to full-week courses.

Guest Houses

Most Grand Cayman guest houses provide modest accommodations, but are a good choice for those seeking more personal lodgings or for those with a close eye on the budget.

ENTERPRISE BED AND BREAKFAST
Selkirk Dr., Red Bay
☎ 345/947-6009, fax 345/716-8380
Reservations: ☎ 818/716-8380, fax 818/348-0433
http://home.earthlink.net/~enterprise
Inexpensive

Star Trek buffs, here's one for you. The theme of this B&B is the famous TV series. Rooms include a double and a twin bed (just one room has a queen bed), air-conditioning, private bath, TV, microwave, small refrigerator, bar sink, dining table and chairs, and a patio or balcony. Facilities include a freshwater rinse station for scuba gear.

Credit cards are not accepted; smoking is not permitted.

For reservations, contact the booking office at the above phone number or write for reservations: 5160 Llano Drive #I, Woodland Hills, CA 91364.

ERMA ELDEMIRE'S GUEST HOUSE
South Church Street
George Town
☎ 345/949-5387, fax 345/949-6987
Inexpensive

Located one mile south of George Town, this guest house is a 10-minute walk from Smith Cove.

Credit cards and checks are not accepted. A three-day deposit is required with reservation.

Rooms include private bath, air-conditioning and ceiling fan. Guests have access to a refrigerator and hot plate (studios and the apartment have private kitchen facilities). Daily maid service except on Sunday.

Live-Aboard Boats

If you are a dedicated diver, you might want to check out one of the live-aboards – floating hotels that literally cruise from one dive site to another. You'll spend a week with others who share your interest. You won't waste time reaching dive sites; what seems like your personal yacht for the week just whisks you there and in you go!

CAYMAN AGGRESSOR III
PO Box 10028
George Town, Grand Cayman
☎ 345/949-5551, fax 345/949-8729
Reservations: ☎ 800/348-2628
www.aggressor.com
Deluxe

This George Town-based 110-foot live-aboard has five professional staff members and takes a maximum of 16 guests at any time. In operation for 12 years, this operator is PADI, NAUI, SSI, NASDS, and YMCA affiliated and offers photo and video rentals. Divers enjoy sites off all three islands. This is an all-inclusive option.

LITTLE CAYMAN DIVER II
☎ 813/269-4542, fax 813/269-2742
Reservations: ☎ 800/458-BRAC
Deluxe

Based off Little Cayman, this live-aboard accommodates 10 passengers in five cabins. Each cabin comes with its own private bath. PADI, NAUI, SSI, NASDS, and YMCA affiliated. In business for 10 years. Offers video rentals.

CAYMAN DIVING LODGE

PO Box 11
East End
Grand Cayman
☎ 345/947-7555, fax 806/798-7568
Reservations: ☎ 800/TLC-DIVE
www.divelodge.com
Deluxe

This all-inclusive live-aboard is located on the
East End of the island, on land. It operates like
a land-based live-aboard and includes all services from meals to dives to taxes.

Best Places to Eat

Days spent shopping for Rolexes and or
diving tropical reefs can end sipping
Dom Perignon and enjoying a meal
prepared by a Cordon Bleu-trained chef.

After a day of shopping, watersports, or beach
fun, many travelers look to the island's fine dining as the evening's entertainment. Caymanian
cuisine reflects the riches of the sea. Fine dining is very much a part of the Cayman experience and an important nightlife option. Casual
dining and restaurants featuring Caribbean
cuisines are other possibilities.

With residents and visitors from around the
world, however, the Cayman Islands also offer
many types of cuisine, especially on Grand
Cayman.

Traditional Caymanian Foods

Turtle, brought to the table in the form of soup, stew, or steak.

Conch, a versatile dish as an appetizer in the form of fritters, a soup prepared as a chowder or thick with onions and spices as a stew, or even uncooked, marinated in lime juice as ceviche.

To sound like a local, pronounce conch as konk.

Pepperpot soup, a savory soup made with greens and potatoes.

Fish rundown, fish simmered in coconut milk with breadfruit and cassava (the source of tapioca).

The influences of nearby Jamaica are seen on island menus as well, especially in the jerk seasoning that ignites fish, chicken, and other meats.

Favorite Caribbean Dishes & Foods

Rice and peas: rice and red beans cooked in coconut milk.

Jerk: Spicy barbecued fish, chicken, goat, or beef; spiced with Scotch bonnet pepper, nutmeg, allspice, and more and cooked over pimento wood.

Breadfruit: Similar in taste to a potato, and served in as many ways.

Fish tea: A broth-like soup.

Johnny cake: Fried bread.

Patty: A meat pie that's a Caribbean standard as popular as an American hamburger.

Pumpkin soup: Made by using Caribbean pumpkins, which are not sweet.

Saltfish: Dried and salted codfish.

Ackee: A fruit that tastes somewhat like scrambled eggs and, for breakfast, is served with saltfish.

Money Matters

Visa, Mastercard, American Express, Diners Club, and Access are commonly accepted; Discover is accepted at some establishments.

Some restaurants add a 15% gratuity to the bill, so make sure you don't tip twice.

In the restaurant department, Grand Cayman has definitely got something for everyone, whether your tastes run toward fresh island seafood or cuisines from around the world. Some of the island's restaurants have received many accolades over the last few years and gained quite a following among the many returning guests who frequent the island; others are new on the scene. Some are especially suited for couples looking for a special night out; others welcome families looking for dishes to please even the pickiest eater in the group.

Typically, vacationers should expect to pay about US $45-75 per person for a three-course meal with wine in one of the island's finest restaurants. Travelers should expect to spend about US $6-10 for a casual lunch or dinner. Fast-food lunches or snacks can be obtained for about US $3-7 per person. Price estimates given below are per person, in US dollars.

Alive Price Scale - Restaurants

Expensive . . . . $40+

Moderate . . . . $25-$40

Inexpensive . . . . Under $25

Fine Dining

CASA HAVANA RESTAURANT
Westin Casuarina, Seven Mile Beach
☎ 345/945-3800
Moderate

Menu selections: glazed swordfish, roast pork tenderloin, and filet mignon.

The Casa Havana is the signature restaurant of the Westin, complete with white-glove service and a romantic atmosphere. Reservations are suggested. The dress is casually elegant.

CASANOVA RISTORANTE
Old Fort Building, George Town
☎ 345/949-7633
Moderate

Menu selections: penne alla grappa prepared with Italian pancetta, sage, rosemary, grappa & tomato sauce.

Specializing in romantic dining, this restaurant is decorated with Italian artwork. An extensive menu offers penne pasta sautéed with Caribbean lobster, linguine with clams, potato dumplings with homemade pesto sauce, veal piccata, and many seafood dishes. Open for lunch Monday through Saturday; dinner nightly. Reservations suggested.

GRAND OLD HOUSE
South Church St., George Town
☎ 345/949-9333
Expensive

The Grand Old House is one of Grand Cayman's most lauded restaurants, and with good reason. We dined here one evening as a wedding reception took place under a huge tent set up on the grounds – it was beautiful.

The Grand Old House is indeed both grand and old, dating back to 1908 when it was built by a merchant and lawyer from Boston. Once surrounded by a coconut plantation, the house was used for entertaining and lavish parties in its early days; later the structure became a hospital for soldiers wounded in World War II and a storm shelter during hurricanes.

Today the home showcases the work of Chef Kandathil Mathai, who has cooked for Prince Charles, Princess Diana, Margaret Thatcher, Princess Anne and the Reagan family. The menu includes entrées such as tenderloin of black Angus beef; New Zealand baby rack of lamb; pork Zurichoise with mushrooms, Chardonnay cream sauce and roasted potatoes; baked filet of dolphin; and potato-crusted tuna.

House specialties are lobster tail sautéed with shallots, mushrooms, fresh tomatoes and beurre blanc; baked shrimp "Grand Old House," cooked with fresh local herbs, white

This restaurant has been given 10 awards by Wine Spectator *magazine.*

wine, and served with Hollandaise sauce; turtle steak Cayman-style; pan-fried crispy duck breast flamed in Cointreau accompanied by a gateau of sweet potato; and wiener schnitzel with spatzle and red cabbage. The dishes are accompanied by an extensive wine list.

The restaurant is open for lunch Monday through Friday from 11:45 to 2 and dinner Monday through Saturday from 6 to 10. Reservations are required.

MAXIN'S FRENCH & CARIBBEAN RESTAURANT

Menu selections: pasta filled with shrimp, served with tasty wild mushrooms in a tomato and saffron sauce.

Fort St., George Town
☎ 345/949-5747
Moderate

Local and French Food with an innovative twist. Lunch is served 10-3, dinner 6-10:30 pm.

RISTORANTE BELLA CAPRI

West Bay Rd., Seven Mile Beach
☎ 345/945-4755
Moderate

Menu selections: fettucine alfredo, seafood linguine & veal parmigiana.

Enjoy seafood or Italian specialties at this casual eatery serving a well-rounded menu of lasagne, veal, seafood, lobster, and steak.

Open for lunch 11:45 to 2 pm on weekdays; dinner 5:30 to 10:30. Reservations are suggested.

BENJAMIN'S ROOF
SEAFOOD RESTAURANT

West Bay Rd. at Coconut Place, Seven Mile
Beach
☎ 345/947-4080
Expensive

When you're ready to go all out, head to this elegant restaurant which serves clams casino,
marinated conch, turtle steak, lobster, shrimp,
crab, scallops, and a full line of meat and pasta
dishes, including NY strip, lamb chops, chicken
cordon bleu, and fettucine alfredo. Don't miss
the lobster Churchill, cooked in white wine and
a mustard sauce.

Benjamin's is the
only place on the
Cayman Islands
to serve alligator
tail.

Open for dinner from 5:30 to 10:30; an early
bird menu is available 3 to 5:30.

EDOARDO'S

At Coconut Plaza, Seven Mile Beach
☎ 345/945-4408
Moderate

This restaurant has been a Cayman fixture for
a decade. It serves fresh seafood, pasta dishes,
and gourmet pizzas made by Chef Randall
Burns.

LANTANA'S RESTAURANT AND BAR

West Bay Rd., Seven Mile Beach
☎ 345/947-5595
Expensive

Save Lantana's for a special evening out during
your vacation. We love the innovative cuisine
served at this elegant restaurant. The chef
offers an excellent menu featuring spicy Cuban

Menu selections: roasted lobster tail with asparagus risotto, red pepper and pesto-crusted salmon, pan-seared grouper, walnut-crusted pompano served with a coconut curry sauce.

black bean soup, jerk pork tenderloin, grilled yellowfin tuna with cilantro linguine, and more, followed by tropical coconut cream pie with white chocolate shavings and mango sauce, or frozen Cayman lime pie with raspberry sauce and whipped cream.

THE LINKS RESTAURANT

The Links at Safehaven Golf Course
☎ 345/949-5988
Expensive

Located upstairs in the golf club, this air-conditioned restaurant is a favorite with duffers for both lunch and dinner. The lunch menu offers fried scampi, fish and chips, burgers, and steaks. Dinner includes a wide variety of dishes, from salmon steak to Jamaican jumbo shrimp to veal schnitzel and Brazilian pork.

Menu selections: filet mignon, Brazilian pork, rack of lamb, lobster.

Open for lunch from 11:30 to 2:30; dinner 6 to 9:30.

THE LIGHTHOUSE

Breakers
☎ 345/947-2047
Moderate to Expensive

Menu selections: lamb chops, chicken Marsala, veal romana with vodka in Gorgonzola cream sauce.

As its name suggests, this eatery is housed in a lighthouse. It's located on the East End – a bit of a drive for most, but worth the effort. Here you can enjoy lunch and dinner either indoors or outside. Serves conch chowder, jerk shrimp pitas, and seafood Caesar salads. Several Italian dishes are offered as well.

LOBSTER POT
North Church St., George Town
☎ 345/949-2736
Expensive

This second-floor restaurant, built with a view of the George Town Harbour, serves up seafood accompanied by an extensive wine list.

Save this one for a special night out; prices are high, even by Cayman standards.

Menu selections: lobster and surf and turf are favorites, as well as grilled salmon filet, mango chicken, Cayman turtle steak, cracked conch, and seafood curry.

Informal Dining

ALMOND TREE
North Church St., George Town
☎ 345/949-2893
Moderate

Since 1973 this restaurant has specialized in local cuisine served in a true island atmosphere. Opt for a patio table if at all possible and sit in the shade of breadfuit, guinip, poinciana and almond trees.

Menu selections: almond snapper, filet mignon, Jamaican pork tenderloin, mango shrimp.

BLUE PARROT
South Church St. at Coconut Harbour, George Town
☎ 345/949-9094
Inexpensive to Moderate

Not necessarily the place to go for a quiet dinner, this restaurant boasts the island's largest TV screen. Order up grilled seafood, sandwiches, and salads for lunch and dinner.

BILLY'S PLACE
North Church St., George Town
☎ 345/949-0470
Inexpensive

This fun eatery is a good introduction to Cayman cuisine.

Favorites include fish Cayman-style, jerk conch or pork, conch stew, ox tail, and stew beans. Jerk chicken pizza, jerk blue marlin, jerk burgers and tandoori shrimp are other popular dishes. Indian dishes such as curried chicken, shrimp or goat, and chicken tikka (marinated chicken baked in a clay oven) round out the menu.

Open for lunch and dinner Monday through Saturday; dinner only on Sundays.

CAFÉ TORTUGA

This restaurant is owned by Tortuga Rum.

West Bay Rd., Seven Mile Beach
☎ 345/949-8669 or 949-7427
Moderate

Menu selections: Many Caribbean favorites such as jerk chicken with rice and peas along with steaks, burgers, pizza, pastas, fish burgers.

Sit inside in the faux-Caribbean atmosphere or outdoors on a very faux-sand "beach" and enjoy reasonably priced breakfast, lunch, or dinner.

❖ **TIP**

Your dessert should include a slice of their not-to-be-missed Tortuga Rum cake.

Service here can be glacial, but reasonable prices make it worth a visit.

CALICO JACK'S
North Church St., George Town
☎ 345/949-4373
Moderate

Dine under the light of the stars at this fun eatery located behind Calico Jack's Pirate Emporium. A weekly barbecue serves up chicken and all the fixin's. Burgers are a favorite.

The nightly tarpon feeding is a good reason to stay a little longer.

CAPTAIN MORGAN'S STEAKHOUSE
West Shore Centre (near Hyatt), Seven Mile Beach
☎ 345/949-2333
Moderate

This fun eatery is known for its tabletop grills, where you cook your own steak. Other menu offerings include Caribbean lobster tail, shrimp, tuna, chicken, turtle steak, and swordfish, all served with baked potato, corn, and salads.

THE COFFEE BAR
The Strand Shopping Centre, George Town
☎ 345/949-6850
Inexpensive

This coffee bar is a favorite spot for breakfast, which starts at 7 am. New York bagels, homemade quiche, croissants, muffins, cinnamon rolls and full breakfast platters with egg, bacon and cheddar are all accompanied by a large selection of international coffees. Daily gourmet lunch specialties available.

CROW'S NEST
South Church St., George Town
☎ 345/949-936
Moderate to Expensive

West Indian favorites fill the menu here. Start with conch fritters or a jerk chicken sampler and then enjoy red bean soup or conch chowder. Entrées include Jamaican chicken curry, Turtle Farm steak topped with a peppery cream vermouth sauce, and red snapper, mahi mahi, mako shark, or swordfish prepared grilled, pan-fried, or blackened. Open for lunch Monday through Saturday, dinner daily.

EATS CROCODILE ROCK CAFÉ
Falls Shopping Mall on West Bay Rd., Seven Mile Beach
☎ 345/947-5288
Inexpensive

This American-style diner starts with a full breakfast.

❖ **TIP**

Don't miss the strawberry-topped French toast!

Menu selections: barbecued baby back ribs, tuna salad sandwich, chili burger.

Daily lunch specials include burgers, soups, salads, sandwiches and fajitas. Dinner offerings include stir-fry dishes, steak, seafood, fajitas, and pasta.

FERDINAND'S CARIBBEAN CAFÉ
Westin Casuarina, Seven Mile Beach
☎ 345/945-3800
Moderate

Named for King Ferdinand, this casual restaurant features Caribbean dishes as well as sandwiches and breakfast. You can dine indoors or outside.

Menu selections: seared tuna and sugarcane grouper.

★ DID YOU KNOW?
The culinary team for the Westin was awarded 21 titles in the 1997 Cayman Island's Culinary Competition.

GOLDEN PAGODA
West Bay Road, Seven Mile Beach
☎ 345/949-5475
Inexpensive to Moderate

Chef's specialties include roast pork with green beans; pork ribs in black bean sauce; shrimp in lobster sauce; and beef with snow peas. Carryout available.

Menu selections: seafood, Chow Choy, soups, curried dishes, and more.

HEMINGWAY'S
Hyatt Britannia Beach Club
West Bay Rd., Seven Mile Beach
☎ 345/945-5700

This is a delightfully fun eatery, located right on the beach with indoor and outdoor seating. Start with pepperpot soup or conch and clam chowder but don't miss the Cayman-style conch fritters with chipotle tartar sauce.

Entrée selections: spiny Caribbean lobster tail, roasted rack of lamb with an herbed cous cous and Caribbean ratatouille, pan-fried snapper on a zesty cous cous and with a sweet pepper essence.

CAPTAIN BRYAN'S PATIO BY THE SEA

The restaurant is noted for Irish jam sessions and dart tournaments.

North Church St. at Mary St., George Town
☎ 345/949-6163
Moderate to Expensive

We enjoyed a great sunset meal out on the patio of this casual eatery. Most appetizers and entrées are prepared with an island flair, such as a red conch chowder that's a meal in itself, pan-fried red snapper, "seafood pasta from hell" (shrimp, scallops, lobster and fish in a hot and spicy citrus sauce), and favorites like coconut shrimp.

Don't miss the conch fritters here!

Make reservations for seats on the patio.

ISLAND TASTE RESTAURANT & LOUNGE

Church St., George Town
☎ 345/949-4945
Moderate

Menu selections: fettucine alfredo, lobster tail, lobster Cayman-style.

We have good memories of a lunch here, enjoyed under the thatched roof during a pouring rainstorm. This open-air, second-floor restaurant is across the street from the *Atlantis* submarine office. Specializing in tropical and Mediterranean cuisine, the menu includes a wide variety of pasta dishes as well as conch steak, dolphin, snapper, and a daily captain's catch. Save room for the key lime pie. Open for lunch and dinner. All-you-can-eat shrimp is available nightly.

LONE STAR BAR
West Bay Rd., Seven Mile Beach
☎ 345/945-5175
Inexpensive to Moderate

Lone Star was named one of the "World's Top 100 Bars" by Newsweek magazine.

This bar is located by the Hyatt Regency entrance.

The atmosphere is rollicking and fun, a mix of both locals and vacationers who come to enjoy a drink and some conversation in this T-shirt decorated bar. The restaurant specializes in Tex-Mex food. Monday and Thursday are all-you-can-eat fajita nights; on Thursday lobster is served (the specialty of the house). Wednesday brings in steak lovers, Friday is a favorite with prime rib buffs and Saturday is barbecue night.

RISTORANTE PAPPAGALLO
Conch Point Rd., West Bay
☎ 345/949-1119 or 949-3479
Moderate to Expensive

The beauty of this restaurant hints at the specialness of a meal here. A thatched roof, made from over 100,000 thatch palm leaves, shields a building built of bamboo, local stones, and marble. Parrots, cockatoos, and macaws lend their voices to create an exotic atmosphere that's echoed in the setting: the restaurant is perched on the shores of a small natural lake in a bird sanctuary.

Meals here are special as well, featuring Northern Italian cuisine. Homemade pastas, seafood, and fine wines make this restaurant well worth the drive for those staying in the Seven Mile Beach area. Dinner is served from 6 to 10:30 pm daily.

SEAHARVEST
South Sound at Sunset House, George Town
☎ 345/945-1383
Moderate to Expensive

Entrée selections: dolphin cardinale with shrimp and served with a lobster sauce, filet mignon, pork Normand with a creamy mushroom & calvados sauce.

Start with smoked salmon, marinated conch, lobster fritters, or coquille St. Jacques (sea scallops with tomatoes) at this elegant seafood restaurant.

The menu also includes a selection of pasta dishes such as seafood lasagne, chicken parmagiana, and cappellini pompadour, angel hair pasta with sundried tomatoes, basil and black mushrooms.

THE WHARF
West Bay Rd., George Town
☎ 345/949-2231
http://wharf.ky
Expensive

Menu selections: surf 'n turf, NY sirloin, Caribbean lobster tail, Cuban black bean soup, grilled Cayman turtle steak, grilled shrimp Provençale.

Just past George Town at the start of the beach, The Wharf is a favorite with couples. This seaside restaurant and bar is open for lunch on weekdays and dinner nightly with a menu featuring continental and Caribbean cuisine, but the Wharf is best experienced as a sunset spot. Located right on the water's edge, the open-air bar offers an uninterrupted view of the setting sun. A school of huge tarpon lingers below the deck, waiting for scheduled handouts, and live music is offered most evenings.

Dining At Rum Point

RUM POINT RESTAURANT
Rum Point
☎ 345/947-9412
Moderate to Expensive

Open for dinner only, this eatery features island favorites like shrimp, lobster, and conch as well as pasta dishes, prime rib, and chicken.

WRECK BAR AND GRILLE
Rum Point
☎ 345/947-9412
Inexpensive to Moderate

Dine on burgers, club sandwiches, patties, conch fritters, BBQ chicken salad, fisherman's salad, and jerk pork sandwiches in the comfort of your bathing suit. Table service to the beachside picnic tables makes this an enjoyable way to lunch on a relaxing Rum Point day.

Dawn to Dusk

The Cayman Islands has long been synonymous with **scuba diving**, but this destination also presents plenty of other types of fun in the sun. However you may define soft adventure – walking, birding, golf, hiking, snorkeling, bicycling, fishing, or horseback riding – Grand Cayman offers professional assistance, rental facilities, and even instruction for those new to the sport.

Although these islands are tops in the scuba world, non-divers will find plenty of activity both in and out of water. **Snorkeling** is a popular pastime and an excellent way to enjoy the area's marine wonders.

Watch your fins while snorkeling or diving; don't kick corals, fans or sponges.

The fish seen in these waters also attract **anglers** from around the globe. Visitors can participate in a deep-sea charter or try their luck with reef or bonefishing. Bonefishing guides are found on each of the three islands.

Sailing excursions, from rollicking "pirate" cruises to tranquil sunset sails, are popular on Grand Cayman. Most include hotel pickup. Do-it-yourselfers can also rent watercraft, including Hobie cats, waverunners, and Sunfish. **Windsurfers** generally head out to either Seven Mile Beach or Grand Cayman's East End, considered the most challenging for advanced windsurfers. And for those who want to glide along but let someone else do the work, **parasailing** operators are found along most of Seven Mile Beach.

Golfers are challenged at two courses on Grand Cayman. The Links at SafeHaven is the only championship 18-hole golf course in the Cayman Islands. At the Hyatt Regency Grand Cayman, the Jack Nicklaus-designed Britannia course can be played an 18-hole executive course, a nine-hole championship course, or an 18-hole Cayman Ball course. Designed to go only half as far as a regular ball, this tricky ball make the best use of the small course area on the island.

Britannia is the world's first course designed for use of the Cayman Ball.

Bird lovers flock to each of the Cayman Islands for a chance to see approximately 200 species ranging from tiny hummingbirds to Cayman parrots to the magnificent frigate bird with a wingspan of seven feet.

If you're looking for something more in the spectator realm, you'll find that too. Take a ride on a real submarine, tour a turtle farm, shop 'til you drop, stroll a verdant botanical garden, or explore historic districts. The choices are enough to satisfy any visitor.

Beaches

Smiths Cove

Although often considered a snorkel site, Smiths Cove on South Church Street just south of George Town is an easy shore dive as well. The reef starts just a few feet from the surface and divers can also explore the West Wall from this location.

All beaches in the Cayman Islands are public.

Snorkelers will find a good spot just south of **Smiths Cove Park**, along South Church street. This free park has good snorkeling among the rocks on its north side; covered picnic tables and plenty of shade make this a popular lunch site as well. **Eden Rock** is also frequented by snorkelers. Another favorite is **Soto's Reef**, sometimes called Passion Reef, located behind Soto's Dive Shop (below the Lobster Pot restaurant on North Church Street). One of the top snorkel destinations is the wreck of the *Cali*. Located a short swim from Calico Jack's in just 20 feet of water, this wreck is a good opportunity for snorkelers to view a wreck site, an experience usually reserved for advanced scuba divers.

★ **DID YOU KNOW?**

Touching coral causes the organism to die.

Seven Mile Beach

At just 5½ miles long, Seven Mile Beach may be somewhat of a misnomer, but in some ways the strip of sand seems much longer because of the numerous businesses packed along its expanse. This beautiful swath of white sand separates hotels, condominiums, and restaurants from an aquamarine sea. Dotted with casuarina trees, this beach is the most popular spot on the island. Come here to watch and be watched, to enjoy an island concoction or to slather on oil and bake yourself into tropical bliss. Watersport operators line the way, offering active sorts anything from scuba trips and parasailing to windsurfing and jetskiing.

Seven Mile Beach runs south to north along Grand Cayman's western edge, stretching from George Town to a region called West Bay. Along Seven Mile Beach, Grand Cayman narrows to a skinny stretch about a nile wide, bordered by the beach on the west and North Sound to the east. On its eastern boundary the sea etches into the land with salt creeks and marsh harbors. Much of these eastern reaches are covered with swampy vegetation.

Along Seven Mile Beach you'll find a public beach park tucked north of the Westin Casuarina Hotel. With plenty of parking (other beach access areas offer parking on the shoulder of busy West Bay Road), this is one of the best options for enjoying Seven Mile Beach if you're not staying at one of the area properties. The park includes shaded pavilions, restrooms with changing rooms, and a small playground for the kids. Squeaky clean and, like the rest of the island devoid of beach vendors, the park is a wonderful place to spend an afternoon.

Spotts

Located east of George Town, Spotts is home to a public beach park with shallow swimming.

Breakers

Also east of George Town, the community of Breakers is home to another public beach park.

Rum Point

The tip of the East End is Rum Point, a peninsula that's home to casuarina trees, chalky sand, aquamarine waters, and a club with just about every watersport imaginable. Recently over $5 million in improvements were made to this getaway spot, which now sports a full-service dinner restaurant, casual lunch eatery and bar, decks and walkways, plenty of comfy hammocks and picnic tables, a gift shop, and more.

The price drops to CI $4 each way for 5:30, 7:30 and 9:30 pm departures.

You can arrive at Rum Point by car (about an hour's drive from George Town) or on the *Rum Pointer Ferry*, which departs from the Hyatt Regency Grand Cayman. This 120-passenger ferry travels to Rum Point in about 30 minutes. For ferry reservations, ☎ 345/947-9412. Ferry tickets are CI $6 each way; children aged five-12 CI $3 each way (children under age five travel free).

If you're at Rum Point at dusk, don't miss the fish feeding off the docks.

★ DID YOU KNOW?

Nude bathing is prohibited in the Cayman Islands and beaches require tops for female bathers.

Scuba Diving

Even among the "been there, done that" scuba crowd, Grand Cayman is a winner. Travelers lucky enough to visit the island will find a wealth of dive sites.

The Cayman Islands are universally recognized as a top dive destination. Since 1957, with the founding of the Caribbean's first dive operation on Grand Cayman, these islands have caught the attention of the diving world. Bob Soto established this first Cayman dive operation and today over 40 dive operators provide service on the three islands.

An average one-tank dive costs about US $35-45.

Over 200 sites lure divers of all abilities, from beginners looking for shore excursions and shallow reef dives to advanced divers looking for wreck and cave explorations. You'll find professional assistance from dive operators on each of the three islands, including resort courses where you'll have the opportunity to sample diving after a one-day course. Full certification courses will award you a "C" card, and advanced courses to teach you the use of scuba computers, the skills of drift diving, and even underwater photography.

Grand Cayman offers approximately 130 dive spots, many less than half a mile from shore. The island is surrounded by approximately 60 miles of dropoffs. One of the most popular shallow dive sites is **Stingray City** on the North Sound; this 12-foot dive is memorable for the southern Atlantic stingrays that divers and snorkelers can hand-feed.

Incredible visibility, measured at 100 to 150 feet, helps make these islands such spectacular dive destinations. With year-round water temperatures of 77 to 83°, visitors can dive comfortably and enjoy an underwater playground that's filled with marine life.

★ DID YOU KNOW?

The Cayman Islands Watersports Operators Association (CIWOA) estimates that about one third of all overnight visitors are scuba divers and about 80% enjoy some form of watersports during their stay. About a quarter of all cruise ship passengers to the Cayman Islands partake in watersports.

Why is Cayman So Popular?

The reasons are many:

- ❖ Dive sites start close to shore in shallow water (25 to 60 feet).

- ❖ A variety of dive experiences are available, for beginners as well as advanced divers.

- ❖ Quality dive operations are found throughout the islands.

❊ Instruction is readily available through any of the certification agencies (PADI, NAUI, SSI, NASDS, and YMCA).

❊ Green sea turtles are often sighted on dives.

❊ Scuba instruction is available in many languages.

❊ Much of the marine life is approachable, such as the rays at Stingray City.

❊ Visibility is excellent year-round.

❊ The leeward side of each island ensures calm waters (dive operations are so confident of this that many guarantee diving 365 days a year).

❊ Strict conservation laws have protected the reefs.

❊ The Caribbean's oldest underwater photography school is located here.

❊ A hyperbaric recompression chamber is available 24 hours a day.

It's the Law!

Strict marine conservation laws ensure the safety of the reefs and the marine life. Dive sites are protected with permanent moorings (over 200 in the islands) so boats can moor rather than anchor and risk damage to the fragile reefs.

Dive Operators

Dive operators emphasize good neutral buoyancy techniques to prevent damage to the corals because of improper positioning in the water.

With Grand Cayman's small size, many divers are picked up in complimentary shuttles by operators on other parts of the island.

All tel. numbers given here are area code 345, unless indicated otherwise.

Abanks Watersports	☎ 945-1444
Ambassador Divers	☎ 800/648-7748
Aquanauts Ltd.	☎ 800/357-2212
Bob Soto's Diving	☎ 800/BOB-SOTO
Capitol's Surfside	☎ 949-7330
Capt. Marvin's Aquatics	☎ 800/550-6288
Cayman Diving School	☎ 949-4729
Cayman Marine Lab	☎ 916-0849
Clint Ebanks Scuba Cayman	☎ 949-3873
Crosby Ebanks C&G Watersports	☎ 945-4049
Dive 'N Stuff	☎ 949-6033
Dive Time Ltd.	☎ 947-2339
Divers Down	☎ 945-1611
Divers Supply	☎ 949-7621
Don Foster's Dive Cayman	☎ 800/83-DIVER
Eden Rock Diving Center Ltd.	☎ 949-7243
Fisheye of Cayman	☎ 800/887-8569
Indies Divers	☎ 800/654-3130
Ocean Frontiers	☎ 947-7500
Off the Wall Divers	☎ 947-7790
Ollen Miller's Sun Divers	☎ 947-6606
Parrots Landing	☎ 800/448-0428
Peter Milburn's Dive Cayman	☎ 945-5770

Red Sail Sports	☎ 800/255-6425
Resort Sports Limited	☎ 949-8100
River Sports Divers Ltd.	☎ 949-1181
Seasports	☎ 949-3965
7-Mile Watersports	☎ 949-0332
Soto's Cruises	☎ 945-4576
Sunset Divers	☎ 800/854-4767
Tortuga Divers Ltd.	☎ 947-2097
Treasure Island Divers	☎ 800/872-7552

For those divers who want to eat, sleep, and drink diving, the live-aboard is a good choice. See pages 93-95 for details.

George Town Dive & Snorkel Sites

George Town has a wealth of good dive sites, all easy to reach.

The Black Forest

Beautiful black coral and waving gorgonians make this site indeed seem like the Black Forest. Located at 60 to 100 feet, this wall dive is just off the South West Point. It is not accessible as a shore dive.

Eden Rocks & Devil's Grotto

Eden Rock Dive Shop on South Church Road is the entry point for one of George Town's most popular dive sites. Eden Rock and the Devil's Grotto, about 150 yards from the shore, are shallow dives. Both are a labyrinth of grottos running out from the shore. Eden Rock is popular not only with divers but also with snorkelers who enjoy the easy entrance and a view of the tunnels and often large tarpon. Eden Rock and Devil's Grotto have a depth of 30-50 feet.

Japanese Gardens

Located off the reef at South Sound, just east of George Town, this dive lies 30 to 60 feet below the surface and is often recommended for beginning divers. Like a little bonsai forest, the area is dotted with staghorn corals and is a good site for underwater photographers.

Japanese Gardens includes some good swim-throughs.

Parrot's Reef

Parrot's Reef and nearby Sunset Reef (see below) are just yards from shore. Parrot's Reef has a depth of 30-60 feet.

Smiths Cove

Although often considered a snorkel site only, Smiths Cove on South Church Street just south of George Town is an easy shore dive as well. The reef starts a few feet from the surface and divers can also explore the West Wall from here.

Soto's Reef

Offshore from Soto's Dive Center, this shallow site is also popular with snorkelers.

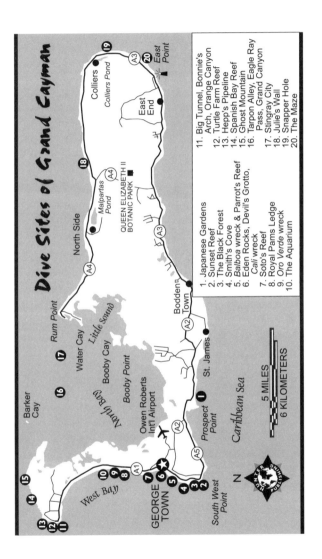

Dive Sites of Grand Cayman

1. Japanese Gardens
2. Sunset Reef
3. The Black Forest
4. Smith's Cove
5. Balboa wreck & Parrot's Reef
6. Eden Rocks, Devil's Grotto, Cali wreck
7. Soto's Reef
8. Royal Pams Ledge
9. Oro Verde wreck
10. The Aquarium
11. Big Tunnel, Bonnie's Arch, Orange Canyon
12. Turtle Farm Reef
13. Hepp's Pipeline
14. Spanish Bay Reef
15. Ghost Mountain
16. Tarpon Alley, Eagle Ray Pass, Grand Canyon
17. Stingray City
18. Julie's Wall
19. Snapper Hole
20. The Maze

Sunset Reef

Just offshore of the Sunset House Resort, this site is a popular stop for divers wanting to do some underwater photography.

The Wreck of the Balboa

The hurricane of 1932 accounted for the wreck of this freighter, which today lies 25 to 40 feet below the surface. Some of the ship is still intact, although parts of it were blown away to clear the traffic channel. This is a popular night dive, offering a manageable depth (during daytime hours, this site sits right in the George Town Harbour waterway, amiking it too busy). Rich with marine life from corals to sponges to brilliant parrotfish, this is one of Grand Cayman's top dive sites.

Wreck of the Cali

Save the *Cali*, located in just over 20 feet of water about 100 feet offshore, for your departure day when you can't scuba dive. It's a great snorkel experience and a good way to finish off your Cayman vacation.

East End Dive & Snorkel Sites

Tucked between Rum Point and West Bay at the mouth of the North Sound lies the island's number one dive site – Stingray City – as well as many other sites for all levels of divers.

Snorkelers will also find that Stingray City is a not-to-be-missed attraction.

Eagle Ray Pass

East of Tarpon Alley and across from the main channel into the North Sound, Eagle Ray Pass is named for the rays that are often sighted here. At 40 to 100 feet, this wall dive appeals divers of varying skill levels.

Grand Canyon

Near the Sandbar west of Rum Point, this 80- to 110-foot wall dive is for intermediate and advanced divers.

Julie's Wall

This dive site lies to the east of the place where Frank Sound Road intersects with the main road. It is 60 to 100 feet below the surface. An intermediate level dive, the wall is home to black coral formations and rays are often spotted here.

The Maze

This is a honeycomb of tunnels that form a veritable maze. It's on the South Channel, not far from the *Wreck of Ten Sails*. This site is 60 to 100 feet below, and is best dived by intermediate and advanced divers as some of the passages lead much deeper.

Snapper Hole

A 30- to 60-foot dive, this is a favorite with beginners but still offers tunnels, plenty of marine life, and even an anchor from an 1872 shipwreck. The site is on the East End outside the reef that forms Colliers Bay.

Stingray City

Just about anyone who has ever heard of the Cayman Islands has heard of Stingray City. This is the top watersports attraction in the Cayman Islands, located in the mouth of North Sound, halfway between the West Bay and Rum Point. Here fishermen once cleaned their catch, attracting large Atlantic southern stingrays which have now become accustomed to being handled by participants in daily snorkeling excursions.

Stingray City got its moniker from Skin Diver *magazine in 1987.*

Stingray City is shared by many watersports operators, who offer half- and full-day excursions that include stops at both deep and shallow spots. Operators depart from all areas of the island for this adventure. The site is now one of the most popular in the Caribbean. Often called "the world's best 12-foot dive," it can be equally enjoyed by both snorkelers and scuba divers.

Truly, this is one experience not to be missed. We have done the Stingray City experience several times using different operators and have never left disappointed. Nothing can quite prepare you for the experience of petting, feeding, and being caressed by the stingrays. The trip out on the North Sound to the site is quick and scenic. After mooring, some vacationers are a little cautious about heading into the waters (the stingrays are far less shy), but we've noticed that all but the most nervous swimmer enjoys this experience.

> ❊ **TIP**
>
> Bring along an old T-shirt to wear on the Stingray City snorkel excursions. Your back is exposed to a lot of sun during this trip and, with the coolness of the water and your excitement over the stingrays, you may not notice you are getting a bad burn. Pack plenty of sunscreen as well.

On the shallow stop, **The Sandbar**, visitors stand (as still as possible to prevent kicking up sand and lowering visibility) while the stingrays swoop by, often brushing participants like some large rubbery Frisbee. Operators begin the feeding and, as visitors become more comfortable with the process, they are allowed to feed and even hold the large rays.

Trips cost about US $45 per person and typically include three stops. The deepest is Stingray City at about 12 feet, followed by the shallower Sandbar, about three feet deep.

Feeding Stingrays

Don't miss the chance to feed the rays some squid. Just pinch the squid between your fingers, arch your fingers back like you're about to slap someone, and put your hand down in the water: the greedy stingrays will do the rest. If you don't arch your fingers back, the rays might suck up your fingers and give you a little scare. They don't have teeth, but their lips are a firm cartilage that will give you a jolt.

Typically about 30 stingrays frequent the area so you're just about guaranteed the opportunity to pet and swim alongside these beautiful creatures.

After feeding the stingrays, most operators then take snorkelers over to **Coral Gardens**, a beautiful snorkel area with several large coral heads, fans, and abundant marine life.

Tarpon Alley

This wall dive of 60 to 100 feet is near Stingray City, just outside North Sound. A favorite with underwater photographers, this site has dropoffs, canyons, and, of course, huge schools of shiny tarpon.

West Bay Dive & Snorkel Sites

The West Bay, located just north of Seven Mile Beach, has many good dive sites. These locations are also very easy to reach for those staying on Seven Mile Beach.

Big Tunnel

Swim-throughs and canyons and a depth of 60 to 100 feet make this a favorite with intermediate and advanced divers. Located off the North West Point (close to Bonnie's Arch and the Orange Canyon).

Bonnie's Arch

Just off North West Point, this 50- to 70-foot dive is a great place for photos because of its arch formation, covered with corals and sponges. Good for beginners, the dive offers even more than the spectacular arch, with many types of marine life, from tarpon to tangs.

Ghost Mountain

At North Point, West Bay, you will see a large coral pinnacle, its base lying on a sand slope at a depth of 140 feet. Large schools of jacks swim in and out of the cave at the base of the pinnacle. This intermediate to advanced wall dive is 70 to 100 feet below the surface.

Hepp's Pipeline

A 30- to 60-foot dive for beginnersi/ntermediate divers not far from the Cayman Turtle Farm. It has two mini-walls and can be a shore dive.

Orange Canyon

A 60- to 100-foot dive, this one is favored by intermediate and advanced levels. Named for its orange elephant ear sponges, the wall is painted with color. Located near Bonnie's Arch.

Spanish Bay Reef

You can walk right out to this shallow reef dive (30 to 60 feet) near Spanish Bay Reef Resort. This site is also good for snorkeling (although the waters can be rough in this area).

Trinity Caves

Look for turtles on this dive.

Located in West Bay, this dive is down 40 to 100 feet. Beginners can enjoy a look at spectacular corals and fans, while intermediate and advanced divers can enter the three channels that wind their way to a wall where larger marine species might be spotted.

Turtle Farm Reef

Just east of the turtle farm, a short swim from the shore, this site offers a steep mini-wall rising from a 60-foot sand bottom. You can do this as a shore dive or enjoy this site as a snorkeler.

Seven Mile Beach Dive & Snorkel Sites

Seven Mile Beach has several good dive sites, although many boats head out from here with divers for sites in George Town or other areas of the island.

The Aquarium

With a name like The Aquarium, this 30- to 50-foot dive has to be good. Look for a wide variety of fish on this dive off the upper end of Seven Mile Beach. Goatfish, snapper, parrotfish, and more await on this beginner-level dive.

Royal Palms Ledge

This site, just offshore from the Marriott, goes to a depth of about 50 feet. There's a tunnel that's a favorite with divers.

Wreck of the Oro Verde

About half a mile off the beach at the site of the former Holiday Inn (soon to be home of a new Ritz Carlton), the *Oro Verde* is a favorite wreck for beginner divers because of its shallow position (25 to 50 feet). The ship was used by drug smugglers and in 1980 was scuttled. Today the gold lies in its rich marine life; the high that divers get from the myriad colors is a completely legal one.

Oro Verde *means "green gold" in Spanish, so we'll let you draw your own conclusions about its cargo.*

A green moray eel named Grumpy was spotted for years at the wreck of the Oro Verde.

Combo Lunch/Snorkel Excursions

 Although these islands are world famous for their diving, many attractions can be enjoyed in water just a few feet deep with a mask and snorkel.

Only yards from shore, even first-time snorkelers can enjoy a look at colorful corals, graceful fans, and fish that include friendly sergeant majors, butterfly fish, and shy damselfish. And travelers shouldn't feel that wreck diving is for scuba divers only. The wreck of the *Cali* is in shallow water and is an easy snorkel trip (see above).

Snorkel excursions are also offered by many dive operators, the most popular being the excursion to Stingray City. Typically these trips include drinks and often lunch following the snorkeling adventure. Complimentary shuttle services are available from some hotels and condominiums.

★ DID YOU KNOW?

Operators will supply snorkels, masks and fins but you don't really need fins for the snorkel excursions. If you are not an experienced snorkeler, fins can be tough to control and you'll run the risk of kicking (and thereby killing) coral formations.

The snorkel excursions on Grand Cayman cover a small area and you can float and admire the marine life without worrying about having to swim hard and keep up with a group.

North Sound Beach Lunch/Snorkel

To learn more about Caymanian life, the North Sound Beach Lunch/Snorkeling trip is offered by several operators. This trip also includes snorkeling at either Stingray City or the Sandbar (depending on visibility and water conditions) and the Coral Gardens, but includes lunch – Cayman-style. The crew dives for pink queen conch, a shellfish that's then prepared as an appetizer, sliced and marinated in lime juice, onion and seasonings like ceviche. Everyone goes on shore at Cayman Kai for a Caymanian lunch of peas and rice, potato or breadfruit salad, and local fish or spicy chicken. Part of the fun is talking with the captain and crew about Caymanian life. These trips cost $50 per person and run from 9 am to 3 or 4 pm.

Combo Lunch-Snorkel Operators

Operators that offer North Sound Lunch/Snorkel trips include:

Abanks Island Adventures	☎ 949-5700
Bayside Watersports	☎ 949-1750
Black Princess Charters	☎ 949-0400/3821
Charterboat Headquarters	☎ 947-4340

All numbers listed here are area code 345 unless indicated otherwise.

Best Value Charters	☎ 949-1603
Capt. Crosby's/C&G Watersports	☎ 947-4049
Capt. Gleason Ebanks	☎ 916-5020/945-2666
Capt. Marvin's Watersports	☎ 947-4500/4590
Cayman Delight Cruises	☎ 949-6738/8385
Dallas Ebanks Watersports	☎ 949-1538/916-2707
Ernie Ebanks Watersports	☎ 949-1538 or 916-2707
Fantasea Tours	☎ 949-2182
Frank's Watersports	☎ 947-5491
Jackie's Watersports	☎ 947-5791
Oh Boy Charters	☎ 949-6341
Stingray City Charters	☎ 949-9200

Sailboating

Sailing excursions are another popular way to enjoy the islands. Charters, sunset cruises, booze cruises, and rollicking "pirate" cruises are offered to entertain vacationers, especially on Grand Cayman. Do-it-yourselfers will find plenty of smaller watercraft: ocean kayaks, Sunfish, Hobie cats, waverunners, and more on Grand Cayman. Rental prices vary by location, but expect to pay anywhere from US $25 to $100 an hour, depending on type of vessel. Catamaran rentals run about $35-$40 per hour.

❈ **TIP**

Interested in learning how to sail? Contact the **Cayman Islands Sailing Club**, PO Box 30513 SMB, Grand Cayman, Cayman Islands BWI; ☎ 345/947-7913, fax 345/947-4383. This sailing club offers sailing classes for all ages.

For a look at the waters off George Town aboard an authentic replica of a 17th-century Spanish galleon, join a cruise aboard the *Jolly Roger* (☎ 345/949-8534). The ship has three masts and 110 pieces of rigging and is thought to be about the size of Columbus' *Niña*.

You'll find many sunset cruises on Grand Cayman; for more see the *After Dark* section (page 189).

Windsurfing

Windsurfing operators are found on Seven Mile Beach and on Grand Cayman's East End. The latter is a top windsurfing area with experienced participants because of its stronger winds. Tradewinds of 15 to 25 knots blow during the winter months, dropping to 10 to 15 knots in the summer.

Windsurfing Operators

There are two dedicated windsurfing operators in Grand Cayman. **Cayman Windsurf** (☎ 345/947-7492), on the East End at Morritt's Tortuga Club, is a BiC Center; beginners are welcome. **Sailboards Caribbean** (☎ 345/949-1068), on Seven Mile Beach, is a Mistral certified school. It also offers ocean kayaks.

Horseback Riding

Horseback riding is an excellent opportunity both to tour some of the island's quieter sections and to romp along the beach. Most horseback riding on the island is along the powdery beaches, an excellent place for practiced riders to gallop and for beginners to enjoy a slow walk on cushioned sand (a comfort to those who feel they may fall off).

Full moon rides are especially popular.

Horseback Riding Operators

Pampered Ponies, ☎ 345/945-2262 or 916-2540.

Honey Suckle Trail Rides, ☎ 345/947-7976 or 916-3363; http://www.horsebackriding.ky.

Nicki's Private Beach Rides, ☎ 345/916-3530 or 945-5839.

Parasailing

Parasailing is a way to truly get a bird's-eye view of Seven Mile Beach. Tourists float up 400 feet above the beach. For information, call **Parasailing Professionals**, Ltd., ☎ 345/916-2953

Fishing

Fishing is more than just a popular activity in Cayman, it's a national obsession. Shore, reef, and deep-sea fishing are available year-round and local guides can provide tackle and point out the best fishing spots on each island.

★ DID YOU KNOW?

The Cayman Islands government encourages the catch-and-release of the blue marlin to help maintain this species in its waters. The government offers free citations to anglers who release their marlin; a form can be obtained from the boat's captain or the charter boat booking office to receive this citation.

Skippers can point anglers to local taxidermists that make nice trophy mounts for a released fish based on its estimated size.

Catch-and-release is encouraged by local captains & applies to all catches that will not be eaten and all billfish that aren't record contenders.

Bonefishing is a top activity. These three- to eight-pound fish are found in shallow flats and afford any angler a good fight on spinning gear.

Reef fishing is also found along the many miles of reefs that surround these islands.

For travelers seeking **deep water** action, charters will gladly take them on a hunt for gamefish, including blue marlin, yellowfin tuna, wahoo, dolphin (dorado) and barracuda. Taking out a charter boat is not an inexpensive proposition, but for many visitors it's the highlight of their trip. A half-day charter begins at about US $400 and may range as high as $1,000 for a full-day trip aboard a large charter with state-of-the art equipment and tackle.

Cayman has some of the strictest marine conservation laws in the Caribbean.

Fly fishing continues to grow in popularity here but anglers should bring all their equipment, as guides and charters do not supply salt-water fly rods.

Golfing

THE LINKS AT SAFEHAVEN
Seven Mile Beach
☎ 345/949-5988, fax 345/949-5457

This is the only championship 18-hole golf course in the Cayman Islands. Summer rates average about US $90 for 18 holes (including cart rental). Shoe rental is available for US $10. Men are required to wear shirts with collar and sleeves; women must wear a shirt to cover shoulders. Golf carts are mandatory and operators must be at least 17 years old and have a valid drivers license. Services at the course include a golf pro for lessons, golf shop, putting greens, chipping and bunker practice areas, aqua driving range, open-air patio bar, and The Links Restaurant for lunch and dinner (see *Best Places to Eat*, page 102).

BRITANNIA COURSE

Hyatt Regency Grand Cayman
West Bay Rd., Seven Mile Beach
☎ 345/949-8020

This Jack Nicklaus-designed course can be played as a nine-hole championship course, an 18-hole executive course, or an 18-hole Cayman Ball course. What's a Cayman Ball course? Well, this is the first one in the world. Designed to go only half as far as a regular ball, the Cayman ball makes the best use of the small course area on the island.

This links-style course, with the challenges of its seaside location, includes blind tee shots, pot bunkers, and two-tiered greens. On the fifth hole, golfers shoot over the Caribbean waters.

Britannia is the first course designed for use of the Cayman Ball.

Tennis

Courts are found at most major hotels and conominium complexes. Many are lighted for night play.

Unique Tours

A Bird's Eye View

**SEABORNE
FLIGHTSEEING ADVENTURES**
☎ 345/949-6029
Hours: call for tour times
Admission

Aerial tours of Grand Cayman are available through Island Air and Seaborne Flightseeing Adventures. The 25-minute tour includes a look at Grand Cayman from a 19-passenger Twin Otter aircraft. Tours are scheduled only from December through June.

"It is a unique way to view the island," said Marcus Cumber, Operations Manager. "We fly at a low level altitude and it is possible to see the stingrays, turtles, and big fish from the sky. We feel that our guides are extremely knowledgeable of the Cayman Islands since they are local residents. We can point out the best of the Islands and discuss the history of the Islands."

Explore the Coral Reef By Submarine

***ATLANTIS* SUBMARINE**
Harbour Dr., George Town
☎ 800/887-8571, 800/253-0493, 345/949-7700
Hours: call for dive times
Admission

If you're curious about what lies below the water's surface, the 48-passenger *Atlantis* submarine is the perfect way to have a peek at Grand Cayman's underwater world. Swimmers and non-swimmers alike enjoy safe, air-conditioned, comfortable travel to 100 feet below the surface aboard the *Atlantis* with a narrated view of coral gardens, sponge gardens, the undersea wall, and more.

❀ TIP

Bring along your camera on this fascinating tour, but load film with an ASA rating of 1000. Your flash is useless in the confines of the sub because it will reflect off the portholes. The ASA 1000 film is fast enough to capture the colorful images you'll witness without using a flash.

Visitors buy tickets at the headquarters located just south of the cruise ship terminal on Harbour Drive in downtown George Town. Tours operate six days a week. The dive takes 50 minutes but the total tour time is 1 hour and 40 minutes. You'll board an open-air boat and travel out to the dive site just off George Town's shore. Bench seating runs the length of the sub and all visitors have a porthole from which to enjoy the underwater scene.

After viewing the marine life, don't be surprised to see some human life forms approaching the submarine... these are the *Atlantis*
divers. Wearing armored wetsuits to protect
against fish nibbles, they feed clouds of hungry
fish and provide good photo opportunities.

*No kids under
three feet tall are
permitted.*

ATLANTIS RESEARCH SUBMERSIBLE
Harbour Dr., ☎ 800/887-8571, 800/253-0493
or 345/949-7700
Hours: five dives daily, Monday through Friday
Admission

Another option is a ride on an *Atlantis* Research
Submersible, also operating from the Atlantis
office on Harbour Drive. Plunging down to a
depth of up to 1,000 feet below the surface, this
vessel offers a one-of-a-kind experience. The 22-
foot sub carries two passengers and a pilot and
is the only vessel of its type open to the public.
Several times a day, it plunges down the
Cayman Wall to depths far beyond the range of
sports scuba divers.

A large, three-foot-diameter convex window
allows the two passengers to sit side-by-side in
front of this viewport. The view varies with the
depth: from 200 to 400 feet below the surface
are colorful sponges and corals in what's
termed the "sponge belt." Hundreds of sponges
blanket the vertical wall in forms ranging from
20-foot-long orange rope sponges to gigantic
barrel sponges. From 650 to 1000 feet, living
formations give way to limestone pinnacles
that house deep-sea creatures such as stalked
crinoids, porcelain corals and glass sponges.

Termed the "haystack" zone, the haystacks or limestone blocks stand over 150 feet tall. Here light no longer penetrates the sea and the research sub illuminates the inky blackness with powerful lights.

The highlight of many trips is a visit to the *Kirk Pride*, a shipwreck that sits on a ledge at 800 feet. This 180-foot freighter sank in a storm in 1976 and its fate was unknown until the wreck was discovered by an *Atlantis* Research Submarine in 1985.

❄ **TIP**

As with the *Atlantis* submarine, bring along your camera; load ASA 1000 film so you will not need a flash.

Advance reservations are strongly recommended for this limited-availability adventure. Be warned that it's a pricey one-hour excursion – US $295 to $395 per person depending on time of dive – but certainly a unique one.

NAUTILUS UNDERSEA TOUR
North Church St., George Town
☎ 345/945-1355
Hours: daily; call for tour times
Admission

The Nautilus offers a one-hour tour to view the rich marine life of the bay. The vessel does not submerge; travelers sit in a glass hull six feet beneath the surface and can go up on deck anytime during the trip, making it attractive for

Good option for those with children.

families with young children. The Nautilus
goes out about three-quarters of a mile offshore,
offering visitors a chance to view two shipwrecks and see a variety of tropical fish. Night
cruises, sunset dinner cruises, and mystery
theater cruises are also available.

SEAWORLD EXPLORER
South Church St., George Town
☎ 345/949-8534
Hours: daily; call for tour times
Admission

*Good for families
with children.*

Actually a glorified glass bottom boat, the
Seaworld Explorer is located next to *Atlantis*
Submarine on South Church Street. Like the
Nautilus, it is a good option for those who might
feel a little claustrophobic about a submarine
adventure (it does not go below the water's surface). Visitors descend into a glass observatory
and view marine life as well as two shipwrecks.
The *Explorer* travels to the *Cali*, a schooner
that hit the reef in 1944, and the *Balboa*, a
freighter from Cuba destroyed by a hurricane.
Today the wrecks are encased in corals and
filled with fish life. *Seaworld Explorer* tours
last one hour.

History Tours

SILVER THATCH EXCURSIONS
Box 344 WB
Town Hall Crescent, West Bay
☎ 345/945-6588
Admission

Two historic tours are offered by Silver Thatch Excursions. The **Eastern Experience** takes travelers to the East End on Grand Cayman. Participants view an old lighthouse and see the Wreck of the Ten Sails Monument, recalling the seafaring days of the Cayman Islands. The tour also stops at Old Prospect, site of the first fort, and Watler's Cemetery. In Bodden Town, participants go on a walking tour to see early Caymanian architecture and then travel on to the Blow Holes at Breakers.

Tour #2 starts with a walking tour of West Bay, including a stop at Old Homestead to learn more about early Cayman life. Travelers then head to George Town for a walking tour of the capital city and a visit to the site of Fort George and Elmslie Memorial Church, built by a shipwright with a ceiling constructed to resemble a schooner's hull. The adjacent cemetery has grave markers that resemble houses, a typical style seen at the island's cemeteries. The tour continues on to Old Prospect and the Old Savannah Schoolhouse.

Both tours are available Monday through Saturday with pickup beginning at 8 am along West Bay Road.

SELF-GUIDED TOURS

Cayman National Trust
☎ 345/949-0445 or 949-5688
Free

The Trust has created walking tours brochures for its most historic districts: West Bay, George

Town, and Bodden Town. These brochures (available for $1 from the museum, National Trust, and visitors information booth) introduce visitors to Caymanian history and architecture and are a wonderful way to learn more about the history that makes these islands special.

Nature Tours

SILVER THATCH EXCURSIONS
Box 344 WB
Town Hall Crescent, West Bay
☎ 345/945-6588
Admission

Geddes Hislop and his wife Janet are the founders of Silver Thatch Excursions, a company that focuses on the history and ecology of the island. Vacationers with an interest in botany can select from two excursions that include the Queen Elizabeth II Botanic Park. One tour follows the **historic route**, traveling to the Old Savannah Schoolhouse, to Bodden Town to see the Slave Wall and Cayman-style homes, and then to the park for a walk along the Woodland Trail. The **Environmental Route** includes bird-watching stops at the Governor Michael Gore Bird Sanctuary and other birding sites and then a tour of the Botanic Park.

Excursions are offered Monday through Saturday with pick up along West Bay Road starting at 8 am. Participants are provided with snacks including traditional Caymanian foods and beverages.

Silver Thatch Excursions also offers specialized **bird-watching trips**. These depart at 6 am on Saturdays and include stops at the Governor Michael Gore Bird Sanctuary, a haven for waterfowl, as well as Meagre Bay Pond, Queen Elizabeth II Botanic Park, and the Willie Ebanks Farm to view endangered West Indian whistling ducks.

MASTIC TRAIL
Cayman National Trust
☎ 345/949-0445 or 949-5688
Admission

Great for bird lovers.

The Mastic Trail is a project of the National Trust. Guided tours travel through a woodland area along a two-mile trail. One of the most interesting areas is a region filled with fine red soil called "red mold." The dirt contains minerals found in the ancient rocks of Africa and scientists believe that, through the years, the dust from the Sahara Desert blew across the Atlantic and the Caribbean to accumulate here. Birders have a chance to sight the Grand Cayman parrot, Caribbean dove, West Indian woodpecker, Cuban bullfinch, smooth-billed ani, and the colorful bananaquit.

The hike also passes 100 different types of trees, including black mangroves that grow from the brackish water, elegant royal palms, and tall mahogany trees. Fruit trees, first planted by early residents, include mango, tamarind, and calabash. Orchids bring color to the trees during the spring season, probably the best time of year to experience this eco-tourism attraction.

Island Sightseeing

Queen Elizabeth II Botanic Garden

Frank Sound Road, East End
Hours: 9 am to 6:30 pm daily
☎ 345/947-3558
www.botanic-park.ky
Admission

This is one of the best attractions on Grand Cayman, both economically and educationally. The garden consists of two attractions: the Woodland Trail and the Heritage Garden. Both offer distinct experiences: one emphasizes Cayman flora and fauna in a natural setting, the other showcases tropical plants from around the globe in a beautiful garden setting.

Located about 25 minutes from George Town, the park comprises 65 acres filled with native trees, plants, and wild orchids, as well as birds, reptiles, and butterflies. The Visitors Centre, Heritage Garden and Garden of Flowering Plants are the newest additions to the gardens. The two-story Visitors Centre, built in traditional Caymanian style, includes displays on natural history and botanical art, and small flower shows. Behind the center, a waterfall leads to a snack bar that serves sandwiches, patties, ice cream and juices.

One of the Caribbean's best gardens.

Visit the **Heritage Garden** for a look at Cayman history. Originally a Caymanian house from the East End, this home has been restored and filled with donated furniture. The three-room structure was once a family home where nine children were raised; today the yard is filled with the plants and fruit trees that a Caymanian family would have grown earlier this century. A cistern collects valuable rainwater and a separated kitchen keeps the heat of the stove (a fire hazard) from the house. Beside the home, gardens contain cassava, sugarcane, plantains, bananas, and sweet potatoes. In small open areas in the lowland forest fruit trees grow in pockets of soil among the ironshore much as they would have generations ago. Medicinal plants commonly grown around a Caymanian house such as aloe vera are found here as well.

Traditional Cayman Housing

Traditional Caymanian houses, like the one at the botanic garden, feature sand gardens. Raked clean, the sand gardens were often trimmed with conch shells and have paths paved with coral. On Christmas Eve, families would replenish the sand in their yard with fresh sand from the beach. No one really knows how the tradition got started but some suspect that, for the early Scottish residents, the fresh white sand reminded them of snow.

The **Garden of Flowering Plants** is the most traditional botanical garden area here, with 2½ acres of floral gardens arranged by color. Pink, purple, orange, silver, and a whole rainbow of tones blossom with color and fragrance year-round. Up high on a site that overlooks the gardens and a small pond that features six-foot Victoria water lilies, a tea house has been constructed.

If you see groups of tiny white butterflies, that means there has been a lot of rain recently. The local name of these tiny insects? Rain butterflies, of course.

The **Woodland Trail**, just under a mile long, is a must-see for anyone interested in Cayman plants. Budget at least half an hour for the walk, but much longer if possible so you'll have the opportunity to read the informative exhibits, stop and listen for the call of a Cayman parrot in the trees, and have time to look for turtles in the swampy undergrowth.

The trail winds through several types of environments. One of the wettest is a buttonwood swamp, filled with its namesake, one of the few trees that can live with its roots continually submerged. The swamp provides humidity for bromeliads and orchids. On the other end of the spectrum, a cactus exhibit illustrates the drier regions of the Cayman Islands, and it's home to large century plants (agave) and cacti. One habitat is similar to that found on Little Cayman and includes flora that grow on the tiny Sister Island.

Watch the shadowy undergrowth and you may spot one of Grand Cayman's shyest residents, the agouti. Other wildlife include the hickatee, a turtle found in the freshwater and brackish ponds of the Cayman Islands and Cuba. The Grand Cayman blue iguana or the Cayman anole lizard with a blue throat pouch are also seen.

Rum Point

Hours: daily
Free (charge for ferry ride)
☎ 345/949-9098

Wonder what Seven Mile Beach might have looked like before all the condos and hotels? Then maybe it's time for a day trip over to Rum Point, a beautiful stretch of beach that's a fun alternative to Seven Mile Beach. Rum Point is located on the East End of the island where the land meets North Sound (home of Stingray City), and is dotted with casuarina trees, chalky sand, aquamarine waters, and a club with just about every watersport. Recently over $5 million in improvements were made to this getaway spot, which now sports a full-service dinner restaurant, casual lunch eatery and bar, decks and walkways, plenty of comfy hammocks and picnic tables, a gift shop, and more.

You can arrive at Rum Point by car (about an hour's drive from George Town) or on the Rum Pointer Ferry, which departs from the Hyatt Regency Grand Cayman. This 120-passenger ferry travels to Rum Point in about 30 minutes. For ferry reservations, ☎ 345/949-9098.

If you're at Rum Point at dusk, don't miss the fish feeding off the docks.

Cayman Turtle Farm

West Bay
Hours: 9-5 daily
☎ 345/949-3893 or 949-3894
Admission

Along with Stingray City, the Cayman Turtle Farm is one of the island's top attractions, drawing in over 260,000 visitors last year. It's the only farm of its kind in the world and for over 30 years this site has offered visitors the chance to get up close and personal with green sea turtles. Allow about 45 minutes to tour the farm.

The turtle farm displays the life cycle of the green sea turtle from birth through the breeding stage. A nursery shows where the eggs, which are laid by the big breeder turtles on a sand beach at the farm, are incubated. The hatchlings live in tanks and are fed a high-protein pelleted diet similar in appearance to dog food. This accounts for the rapid growth of the farm's turtles compared to their relatives in the wild.

Good activity for rainy days.

★ DID YOU KNOW?

Named for the color of their fat, some green sea turtles reach 700 pounds.

The self-guided tour of the turtle farm takes you past many tanks filled with turtles in various life stages. A special tank contains turtles that you may pick up and hold, an excellent photo opportunity. Reach down and clutch the turtle's body just behind his front flippers. He'll flip and flap around, trying to swim away in mid-air, unless you hold him vertically.

The farm also recognizes the land residents of the Cayman Islands in several exhibit areas. Look for the agouti or the Cayman "rabbit" in one area. These rodents found in the eastern districts of Grand Cayman have long, thin legs, hoof-like claws, and three toes on their hind feet (five toes on the forefeet). Once a food source, today the rodents are rarely spotted. Nearby, another display area houses the American crocodile. Early records speak of sightings of this 20-foot crocodile in Grand Cayman and Little Cayman; recent archaeological finds have proven this claim to be true.

The last stop on the walk-through of the farm is the extensive gift shop. You might be shocked to see turtle steak and turtle shells for sale in the shop. Remember, however, that this is a working farm. Many turtles are released into the sea every year, although others find their way onto Cayman dinner tables. Much of the turtle meat served at local restaurants comes from the Cayman Turtle Farm. The farm defends its efforts and points out that by providing turtle meat, a longtime Caymanian favorite, to the local market it diminishes the need for turtle hunting. Also, the survival rate at the farm is much higher than in the wild (here, nine out of every 10 turtles survive, as compared to one out of 10 in the sea).

Nesting season occurs from May through October.

❋ **TIP**

Remember, you cannot bring turtle products back through US Customs. They will be confiscated.

Hell

Ready to go to Hell? Well, here it is, just north of Seven Mile Beach. This odd attraction is actually a community named Hell, a moniker derived from the time an English commissioner went hunting in the area, shot at a bird, missed, and said "Oh, hell." The name must have seemed appropriate for the devilishly pointed rocks near town, a bed of limestone and dolomite that through millions of years eroded into a crusty, pocked formation locally called ironshore.

To reach this small community, follow West Bay Road north from Seven Mile Beach. At the intersection of Town Hall Road, turn right and continue to the intersection of Hell Road. Turn left to this small town.

Today, Hell trades upon its unusual name as a way to draw tourists to the far end of West Bay. Visitors stop at the Post Office (and the three shops directly adjacent) to buy postcards and have them postmarked from Hell. Nearby, **The Devil's Hangout Gift Shop** (open daily) located in the original post office ships out its share of postcards. The store is manned by Ivan Farrington, who dresses as the devil himself to greet tourists who arrive to purchase postcards and other Hell-related gifts, from hot sauces to T-shirts.

Conch Shell House

Interesting as a "drive by" attraction in West Bay, the conch shell house is included on most island tours. It's privately owned so you can't enter the premises, but the North Sound Way attraction is often photographed. Handmade from conch shells, it's charming and certainly one of the most picturesque homes in the Caribbean.

Pedro St. James

Savannah
Hours: 9-5 daily
☎ 345/947-3329
www.pedrostjames.ky
Admission

One of the East End's newest attractions is also its oldest. Pedro St. James Restoration Site, an 18th-century great house, has undergone complete renovation and today the building known as the "Birthplace of Democracy in the Cayman Islands" can be visited. Called Pedro Castle, the historic structure is located in the community of Savannah, east of George Town.

The oldest known stone structure in the Cayman Islands, Pedro Castle was first built in the late 18th century as a great house for William Eden, an early settler. In 1831, the house was the site of an historic meeting when residents decided that the five districts should have representation in the government. Four years later, a proclamation declaring the emancipation of all slaves was read at Pedro Castle and several other sites in the islands.

The restoration has been a major undertaking; a US $6.25 million project to restore the great house took from 1820 to 1840. The site is at the center of a 7.65-acre landscaped park atop the 30-foot Great Pedro Bluff. For the past several years, historic research into the site has been conducted.

Cayman Islands National Museum

Harbour Drive
George Town
Hours: 9-5 Mon-Fri, 10-2 Sat
☎ 345/949-8368
www.museum.ky
Admission

The Cayman Islands National Museum is, in our opinion, one of the finest museums in the Caribbean. A visit here is a great way to learn more about Cayman history and culture. Over the years, this seaside building, just across from the cruise ship terminals, has served as a courthouse, jail, and meeting hall, and today it houses over 2,000 artifacts that recall the history of these islands. Created in 1979 by a museum law and opened in 1990, the museum collects items of historic, scientific, and artistic relevance.

You'll enter on the ground floor, and begin with an eight-minute slide show about the history of these islands. From there, enjoy a self-guided tour of the museum, with displays on all facets of Caymanian life. A bathymetric map displays the depth of the seas around the Cayman

Islands, including the Cayman Trench at 23,750 feet below sea level. Other exhibits feature natural history: mangrove swamps which create a rich birding environment; caymanite, a semi-precious stone unique to the Cayman islands; and displays on local marine life.

★ DID YOU KNOW?

This museum is housed in the Old Courts Building, one of the few 19th-century structures left on the island. Outdoor steps lead up to the second story of the building and those 12 steps gave rise to a Cayman saying: "walking the 12 steps," which meant you were being taken to court.

One of the Caribbean's best museums.

Some of the most fascinating displays recall the early economy of the Caymanians. An oral history program reveals the history of early turtlers who made a living capturing the now protected reptiles. Exhibits show the tools of the early residents such as the muntle, a club used to kill fish, the calabash, a versatile gourd that once dried had many uses, sisal switches used to beat mosquitoes away, and wompers, sandals worn on the East End, originally made from leather and later from old tires.

After your museum tour, you'll exit through the museum shop, a good source of Cayman-made items. The shop, housed in the old jail with part of the old coral stone wall still exposed, has a good selection of books and maps of the Cayman Islands. (If you don't have time for a museum tour, you can enter through the store for a little shopping.)

Cardinal D's Park

Off Courts Rd., George Town
Hours: daily; tours at 11 and 2
☎ 345/949-8855
Admission

This small zoo is a good stop for families. Over 60 species of exotic birds (including Cayman parrots and whistling ducks) as well as agoutis, blue iguanas, turtles, miniature ponies, emus, and more are on display. A petting zoo and snack bar make this attraction popular with kids.

Good choice for families

Mastic Trail

Cayman National Trust
☎ 345/949-0445 or 949-5688
Admission

For over two centuries man has walked the Mastic Trail, which winds for two miles through swamps, woodlands, and farming areas. Originally used to herd cattle to the south coast, today the trail is maintained by the National Trust for the Cayman Islands and is an excellent way for travelers to learn more about the many types of fauna found here.

Guided 2½-hour walks, led by local resident Albert Hines, travel past 100 different varieties of trees and 550 other types of plant species such as the wild banana orchid, the Cayman national flower. Only eight people are permitted on each of the tours.

❈ TIP

The tour is not recommended for children under age six, for the elderly, or for those with physical disabilities. Travelers should wear sturdy shoes and bring insect repellent. Cold soft drinks and transportation back to the trailhead are provided.

Reservations are required; on weekdays call ☎ 345/949-1996 between the hours of 10 am and 3 pm, or e-mail ntrust@candw.ky.

Blow Holes

On main road between Frank
Sound and East End
Hours: anytime
Free

East of the turn-off for Frank Sound Road lies a side-of-the-road attraction: the Blow Holes. Park and walk down to the rugged coral rocks that have been carved by rough waves into caverns. As waves hit the rocks, water spews into the air, creating one of the best photo sites on the island.

You'll access the blowholes from a free parking area just off the main road. Follow the wooden stairs down to sea level. The "blows" are strongest when the waves are large (and don't blow at all on the calmest days), shooting sprays of water 20 to 30 feet in the air.

> ### ☠ WARNING!
> Don't stand too close to the edge of these formations. Wear good shoes for this excursion; the ironshore is sharp and footing isn't solid.

Pirates Caves

Bodden Town
Hours: 9am-5pm
☎ 345/947-3122
Admission

A less scenic and more touristy stop (but nonetheless fun) are the Pirate Caves in Bodden Town. Reputed to have been used by pirates to hide their treasure and supposedly linked by tunnels to similar caves in the reef, the cave is now open for self-guided tours. You'll first view a caged blue iguana and Cayman parrot as well as a traditional Cayman cottage, then head underground for a look at the cave. Across the street, alleged pirate graves, actually carved by slaves from rock in the shape of small houses, await inspection.

Good choice for families with kids.

Stingray Brewery

Red Bay Road, past Prospect
☎ 345/947-6699
Free

This microbrewery produces the Stingray Beer sold throughout the islands and offers a tour of the brewing process. Closed Sunday.

Little Cayman Day Trip

☎ 345/949-5252, 800/9-CAYMAN
Admission

One of Grand Cayman's attractions isn't on the island at all but on Little Cayman. If you'd like to have a look at this Sister Island but don't want to budget for a stay, consider a day trip to Little Cayman. You can depart Grand Cayman for the quick flight to Little Cayman and spend the day sightseeing. The tour includes a look at Blossom Village, the tarpon pond, and the bird sanctuary. You can stop by Little Cayman Beach Resort for lunch and to change into a swimsuit and pick up snorkel gear for a look at the Bloody Bay Wall, Point of Sand Beach, and other sites. After some tennis or a bike ride, take a quick shower and fly back to Grand

Cayman. One- and two-night trips are also available.

Shop Til You Drop

Shopping & Money Matters

The Caymanian dollar carries a fixed exchange rate of US $1.20 to CI $1. The US dollar is also accepted in shops and restaurants, along with travelers checks and most major credit cards. Visa, Mastercard, American Express, Diners Club, and Access are commonly accepted; Discover is accepted at some establishments.

The turtle appears as a watermark on all notes in the Cayman Islands.

Grand Cayman is the fifth largest financial center in the world, with over 500 banks, so currency exchange and ATMs are not a problem.

George Town Shopping

Grand Cayman is one of the Caribbean's great shopping destinations. The capital of the nation's shopping world is George Town. Along the George Town waterfront on West Bay Road and Harbour Drive, duty-free shops tempt travelers with china, perfumes, leather goods, watches, crystal, and, most especially, fine jewelry.

Currency Conversion Chart

US $	to	CI $
1.00		80¢
2.00		1.60
3.00		2.40
4.00		3.20
5.00		4.00
6.00		4.80
7.00		5.60
8.00		6.40
9.00		7.20
10.00		8.00
15.00		12.00
20.00		16.00
25.00		20.00
30.00		24.00
50.00		40.00
75.00		60.00
100.00		80.00
125.00		100.00

CI $	to	US $
1.00		1.25
2.00		2.50
3.00		3.75
4.00		5.00
5.00		6.25
6.00		7.50
7.00		8.75
8.00		10.00
9.00		11.25
10.00		12.50
15.00		18.75
20.00		25.00
25.00		31.25
30.00		37.50
50.00		62.50
75.00		93.75
100.00		125.00
125.00		156.25

Prices average about 25% below regular retail price tags, although some goods run as much as 40 to 45% below US retail prices. However, travelers would be well advised to know their prices before they leave home; not all items are a bargain.

No taxes are charged on purchases.

Jewelry is a top purchase in the form of watches, custom-designed pieces and stones. Diamonds and other gemstones are found in most fine jewelry stores as well as 14K and 18K gold. Jewelry made from antique coins and doubloons recovered from shipwrecks around the world is very popular here.

Caymanite, a stone found only on the eastern end of Grand Cayman's East End and the bluff on Cayman Brac, is sold throughout the islands mounted as jewelry. The semi-precious stone, a form of dolomite, ranges from a light beige to a beautiful amber color and is often mounted in a gold setting.

Black coral jewelry is also a widespread commodity, and artisans design it into fine jewelry and small sculptures. You'll find black coral necklaces, charms, earrings, and more, often highlighted with gold inlays, sold in most of the fine jewelry shops.

Customs Concerns

Harvesting of black coral depletes the sea's supply. Only jewelers licensed to remove the coral may do so and without a certificate testifying that your purchase is from an approved seller your black coral may be confiscated in US Customs.

Travelers in transit through the US need to avoid anything made with turtle products. All goods – including oils, steaks, shells, and jewelry – made from turtles and turtle shells have been banned by US Customs. All in-transit passengers traveling through the US to other nations will have to surrender turtle products at US Customs.

Cayman-produced **rums and rum cakes** are a popular purchase and can be found in many shops. Tortuga Rum Cake, made using five-year-old Tortuga Gold Rum, is sealed in a red tin and is the product of a 100-year-old family recipe. Or, for travelers who want to skip the cake, a bottle of Tortuga, Blackbear, or Cayman Gold Rum makes an inexpensive duty-free purchase.

Local arts and crafts are also popular buys. Birdhouses made from coconuts, brooms woven from thatch, and pepper sauce distilled form fiery Scotch bonnet peppers to capture the spirit of the islands make inexpensive island souvenirs.

The Best Shops

KIRK FREEPORT
Cardinal Avenue, George Town
☎ 345/949-7477

The Kirk Freeport name is a Cayman institution, well-known among for those seeking duty-free gifts.

The best known of the Kirk Freeport stores is Cardinal Avenue's Kirk Jewellers, the exclusive Rolex distributor in the Cayman Islands. The shop also stocks Tag Heuer, Omega, Breitling, Tudor, Gucci, Bulgari, Fendi, and other lines. Fine jewelry from designers such as Bulgari, Mikimoto, Soho, and Chaumet are popular purchases. Writing instruments and leather accessories from Cartier, Mont Blanc, Waterman, and A.T. Cross are also offered at duty-free prices.

Other shops under the Kirk Freeport umbrella include the exclusive Cartier Boutique, which offers 18 karat jewelry, watches, leather goods, perfumes, and pens, and La Perfumerie I & II, featuring fragrances from around the globe, including Chanel, Lancôme, Yves Saint Laurent, Givenchy, Clinique, and more.

Mini-facials and makeovers are also available.

Fine Jewelry & Watches

BERNARD K. PASSMAN'S BLACK CORAL
Fort St., George Town
☎ 345/949-0123

Black coral in the form of fine jewelry as well as sculpture and even cutlery sets are offered in this gallery. Passman was commissioned to create a black coral horse and corgi for Queen Elizabeth II and Prince Philip; his black coral creations are considered works of art.

COLOMBIAN EMERALDS INTERNATIONAL
Harbour Dr., George Town
☎ 800/6-NO-DUTY
www.colombianemeralds.com

This popular Caribbean boutique, with locations in Antigua, Aruba, the Bahamas, Barbados, Grenada, St. Lucia, St. Martin, the USVI and others, sells not only emeralds but other fine gemstones. All purchases include certified appraisals, 90-day insurance and full international guarantees.

DIAMONDS DIRECT
Anchorage Centre, George Town
☎ 345/945-6868

Diamonds are a shopper's best friend thanks to duty-free and tax-free prices at this store, which deals directly with mine sources in Africa and Russia.

DIAMONDS IN PARADISE
Harbour Dr., George Town
☎ 800/94- CARAT
www.dutyfree.com/dip

Offers a good selection of diamonds set in rings, bracelets, earrings and more.

DUTY FREE LTD.
South Church St., George Town
☎ 345/945-2160

This shop, located right on South Church Street just past where Harbour Drive becomes South Church, offers all types of gold jewelry as well as treasure coins, gems, black coral, and watches. Paloma Picasso creations as well as Tiffany and Co. gifts available. Watches from Seiko, Sector, Guess, Bulova and other brands.

JEWELER'S WAREHOUSE
Harbour Dr., George Town
☎ 800/661-JEWEL
http://dutyfree.com/jw

This store has good prices on a variety of fine jewelry, from earrings starting under $100 and small strands of pearls for under $35 to fine gemstones with four-digit pricetags.

LONDON JEWELLERS FACTORY STORE
Anchorage Centre, George Town
☎ 345/949-9861

Fine gems and gold jewelry are the specialty of this outlet store which sells many sample lines and production overruns at a discount price. Along with fine jewelry, this shop sells designer watches by Seiko, Calvin Klein, Festina, Alfex, and Wittnauer.

BRITISH OUTPOST
☎ 345/949-0742

Along with jewelry, this large store is the exclusive agent for Keieer, Sector and Wittnauer watches.

Linen

FAR AWAY PLACES
Shedden Rd., George Town
☎ 345/949-7477

Far Away Places is well known for its linens and lace. Battenberg lace, towels, tablecloths, placemats, and other items fill the shop.

Antiques & Antique Jewelry

ARTIFACTS
Harbour Dr., George Town
☎ ☎ 345/949-2442

This shop specializes in rare coins and coin jewelry but also has a large inventory of silver, antique scientific instruments, West Indian maps, and Halcyon Days enamel works. It's fun to look around their collection of shipwreck coins.

Books

THE BOOK NOOK II
Anchorage Centre, George Town
☎ 345/949-7392

This shop (along with its cousin on Seven Mile Beach) is excellent for its selection of both non-fiction and fiction books. You'll also find a good selection of Caribbean travel books at both (and we were pleased to see our *Adventure Guide to the Cayman Islands* in stock here, too!).

China, Crystal & Figurines

FLAMEWORKS
Anchorage Centre, George Town
☎ 345/945-3122

Located right in the midst of the Anchorage Centre, we spent one afternoon at a table in the mall watching glassmakers create beautiful handmade creations. Stepenn Zawistowski and his assistants create sculptures from small collectibles to full-size marine life.

HOT TROPICS
Anchorage Centre, George Town
☎ 345/949-4514

This perfume shop also sells china by Lenox, Spode, Royal Worcester, Royal Doulton and crystal by Swarovski and others.

KIRK FREEPORT GALLERY
Cardinal Ave., George Town
☎ 345/949-7477

The Kirk Freeport Gallery sells Lalique, Swarovski silver crystal, collectible figurines, Hummel, Lladro, and other fine items. China and crystal collectors can also stop by the **Waterford and Wedgwood Gallery** on Cardinal Avenue.

Housed in a Tudor-style building, this shop includes an extensive collection of Waterford crystal from Ireland and Wedgwood china and crystal from England.

Cigars

CHURCHILL'S CIGAR STORE
Anchorage Centre, George Town
☎ 345/945-6141

Don't forget you can't take Cuban cigars back into the US.

Imported and locally produced Cayman Crown and Cayman Premium cigars are the specialty of this shop. Cohiba, Hoyo de Monterry, Romeo y Juliete, Montecristo and other brands are found here.

The store is the exclusive agent for Davidoff.

Leather Goods

THE COACH FACTORY STORE
Anchorage Centre, Cardinal Avenue off Harbour Drive, George Town
☎ 345/949-5395

Just steps from the cruise terminal, this duty-free shop sells Coach leather goods direct from the factory.

DE BAG MAN
Duty Free Centre, George Town
☎ 345/949-7023

This shop sells a variety of fine leather goods in a range of prices.

KIRK LEATHER STORE
Kirk Freeport Centre
Cardinal Ave., George Town
☎ 345/949-7477

The Kirk Leather Store on Albert Panton Street also sells designer leather goods from Paloma Picasso, Bally, Fossil, Moschino, and Fendi.

Perfumes & Cosmetics

HOT TROPICS
Anchorage Centre, George Town
☎ 345/949-4514

This duty-free shop features perfumes by Dior, Chanel, Lancôme, Clinique, Elizabeth Arden,

Estée Lauder and more. China and crystal also offered.

CARTIER BOUTIQUE

Kirk Freeport stores, Cardinal Ave.,
George Town
☎ 345/949-7477

Mini-facials and makeovers are also available.

This elegant shop offers fragrances from around the globe: Chanel, Lancôme, Yves Saint Laurent, Givenchy, Clinique, and more.

Cameras, Hi-Fi & Audio Equipment

CAYMAN CAMERA, LTD.

South Church St., George Town
☎ 345/949-8359

We were pleasantly surprised by the prices at this good camera store when we ran short of film. Often film prices in the islands are double what you'd find in the States; this shop sells film and accessories for the same price. You can also find batteries and inexpensive underwater cameras here as well as serious photographic gear from Nikon, Hasselblad, Olympus, Minolta, Pentax and others.

SUNSET UNDERWATER PHOTO CENTRE

South Church St., George Town
☎ 345/949-7415

More a lab and rental facility than a retail store, this shop has everything you'd need to start a hobby in underwater photography –

including classes by renowned underwater photographer Cathy Church. The shop offers Nikonos repairs as well as rentals and E6 film processing.

An inexpensive underwater camera is a great purchase while on the island – a wonderful way to record your snorkel trips.

Sunglasses

DE SUNGLASS MAN
The Duty Free Centre, George Town
☎ 345/949-8964

This shop advertises designer sunglasses at 40% off retail prices. Brands include Revo, Ray Ban, Oakley, Maui Jim, Armani, Versace, and others.

Grog & Spirits

BLACKBEARD LIQUORS
Crewe Rd. at Airport Rd., George Town
☎ 345/949-8763
www.blackbeards-liquors.com

Ten flavors of locally produced Blackbeard Rum are sold at several outlets on Grand Cayman. These shops also sell Cuban cigars, coffees, beer, and wines.

TORTUGA RUMS
Selkirk Plaza, ☎ 345/945-7655;
Airport, ☎ 345/949-2258

Premium gold, 151 proof, 98 proof dark rum, and coconut rum are sold by Tortuga Rums as well as Rum Cream and Rum Liqueur. Tortuga

Rums also makes a wonderful rum cake made with gold rum.

Fashion Boutiques

ISLAND CASUALS
Cayside, Shedden Rd., George Town
☎ 345/949-8094

Forget that bright sundress or the super cool shorts? You'll find all that and more at Island Casuals, which specializes in swimwear, polo shirts, casual separates, and tropical print shirts for men, women, and children.

Local Crafts

CARIBBEAN EMPORIUM
Shedden Rd., George Town
☎ 345/949-0466

You won't forget this shop... it literally has a sand floor. Designed to look like a small beach village, the shop sells a good array of food products including Caribbean sauces and marinades as well as crafts, T-shirts, and souvenirs.

HERITAGE CRAFT SOUVENIRS & GIFT MARKET
Harbour Drive and Goring Ave., George Town
☎ 345/945-6041

This shop specializes in Caribbean gifts and souvenirs including straw hats, local music, Caribbean coffees and teas, artwork, hammocks, wood carvings, and more. The shop is located opposite the National Museum, just steps from the cruise terminal.

Gifts & Souvenirs

CAYMAN ISLANDS NATIONAL MUSEUM
Harbour Dr., George Town
☎ 345/949-8368

This shop is a good stop even if you don't have time for a tour of the museum (there's a separate entrance for the store). Housed in the old jail, part of an old coral stone wall is exposed, giving the shop an interesting feel. You can purchase postcards, souvenirs, maps, Caribbean books, and even Caymanite jewelry here.

Art Galleries

PURE ART GALLERY AND GIFTS
South Church St., George Town
☎ 345/949-9133

All types of Caymanian and Caribbean art are showcased, along with a variety of crafts.

Along West Bay Road

Although not as extensive as the shopping in George Town, even the most dedicated shopper will find plenty of diversion along West Bay Road heading up Seven Mile Beach. Coconut

Place, West Shore Center, and Galleria Plaza are some of the top shopping areas. Travelers can look for duty-free liquor, jewelry, island clothing, and other vacation purchases along this strip. The Marriott (formerly the Radisson), Westin Casuarina, and Treasure Island Resort each have numerous shops selling jewelry, resort clothing, and gift items.

Seven Mile Beach Shopping

Fine Jewelry

CHESTS OF GOLD
Hyatt Regency, ☎ 345/949-8846; Westin Casuarina, ☎ 345/949-5330

Numismatic jewelry, diamond creations, and champlevé enamel designs are set in primarily 18 karat gold at these popular shops.

MITZI'S
Bay Harbor Center, West Bay Road
☎ 345/945-5014

Mitzi's specializes in fine jewelry including beautiful gold work by Carrera y Carrera, all in 18 karat gold.

SAVOY JEWELLERS
Queen's Court, West Bay Road
☎ 345/949-7454

A Caymanian favorite, it features an extensive collection of diamonds, Hermes watches, the St. Petersburg Collection of Fabergé eggs, Erté sculptures, and other finery. All jewelry is 18K gold and transportation from island hotels is available upon request.

24-K MON JEWELERS
Treasure Island Resort, ☎ 345/949-9729; Buckingham Square (by Hyatt), ☎ 345/949-1499; Cayman Falls (opposite Westin), ☎ 345/945-7000

Coins, diamonds, gemstones, and gold jewelry are the specialty of these shops. Black coral, pearls, hand-enameled cloisonné, and custom creations.

Antiques & Antique Jewelry

VENTURE GALLERY
West Shore Centre
☎ 345/949-8657

This shop has an array of shipwreck coins and artifacts.

Books

THE BOOK NOOK
Galleria Plaza, West Bay Road
☎ 345/945-4686

This bookstore is one of our favorite stops on Seven Mile Beach. We always find a good selection of Caribbean guidebooks and cookbooks here. Also has a large children's section, including toys for those restless young travelers.

Cigars

CHURCHILL'S CIGAR STORE
Inside De Bag Man
Galleria Plaza, West Bay Road
No phone

This duty-free shop sells Cayman Crown hand-rolled cigars as well as Cohiba, Romeo y Juliete, Montecristo, Hoyo de Monterry, and other imports.

LA HAVANA RESTAURANT & CIGAR EMPORIUM
Queens Court
☎ 345/949-2345

This Cuban restaurant also has a showroom of Cuban cigars – Monte Cristo, Cohiba, Romeo y Julieta and more.

Leather Goods

LE CLASSIQUE SHOE AND LEATHER EMPORIUM
Galleria Plaza, West Bay Road
☎ 345/949-7105

You'll find all styles of duty-free purses and shoes at this shop.

Sunglasses

DE BAG MAN
Galleria Plaza
☎ 345/949-6538

Along with leather goods, this shop sells designer sunglasses by Ray Ban, Revo, Oakley, Armani and others.

Grog & Spirits

BLACKBEARD LIQUORS
The Strand, Seven Mile Shops
☎ 345/949-8763
www.blackbeards-liquors.com

Ten flavors of locally produced Blackbeard Rum are sold at the four outlets on Grand Cayman. These shops also sell Cuban cigars, coffees, beer, and wines.

TORTUGA RUMS
West Shore, ☎ 345/949-4163

Premium gold, 151 proof, 98 proof dark rum, and coconut rum are sold by Tortuga Rums as well as Rum Cream and Rum Liqueur. Tortuga Rums also makes a wonderful rum cake made with gold rum.

Fashion Boutiques

ISLAND CASUALS
Galleria Plaza, West Bay Rd., ☎ 345/945-0924;
Hyatt Regency, West Bay Rd., ☎ 345/945-4359

Specializes in swimwear, polo shirts, casual separates, and tropical print shirts for men, women, and children.

LA PERLA
The Strand
☎ 345/945-4979

This exclusive boutique features La Perla Italian swimwear, lingerie and resortwear.

Gifts & Souvenirs

TROPICAL TRADER
Galleria Plaza
☎ 345/949-8354

This shop claims to be Cayman's largest T-shirt store and they just might be. You'll also find crafts, coffees, island music, and more.

Children's Toys & Clothing

KAYMAN KIDS
Galleria Plaza, West Bay Rd.
☎ 345/945-2356

Clothing and toys in all price ranges and styles are available at this boutique. Among the most interesting items are the Caymanian Cottages, dollhouses designed to look like the cottages of the island. Other items include swimwear, heirloom clothing, hats, and shoes.

Art Galleries

PURE ART GALLERY & GIFTS
Hyatt Regency, West Bay Rd.
☎ 345/945-5633

All types of Caymanian and Caribbean art are showcased in this gallery, along with a variety of crafts. We purchased an inexpensive woven rug with the emblem of the Cayman Islands here; you'll also find a good variety of rum cakes.

After Dark

With its early-to-rise scuba diving crowd, some travelers assume that the Cayman Islands have little nightlife. But more activities now tempt night owls, especially along Seven Mile Beach, from steel drum bands to piano bars.

Live Music

Live music is found at many other bars around the island. Several nightclubs also offer live music and DJ action and are very popular with younger travelers.

The Barefoot Man

Mention Cayman and nightlife in the same sentence and the island's best-known performer comes to mind: the **Barefoot Man**. George Nowak, AKA the Barefoot Man, has been entertaining Cayman audiences for years and his music was heard in *The Firm*. We first saw him at the Holiday Inn Grand Cayman, playing (yes, barefoot) on the sand behind the hotel to a standing-room-only crowd. (When we left later, cars were lining the road for miles on each side of the Holiday Inn, even though he played there most days every week.)

Today, the Holiday Inn is no more now that plans call for the construction of a new Ritz-Carlton on the site and the Barefoot Man has moved on. He can now be found at the Royal Palms Beach Club on Seven Mile Beach. The Barefoot Man and his band play their popular island tunes Thursday through Saturday starting at 8 pm.

LEGENDZ
The Falls Shopping Centre, George Town
☎ 345/945-5288
Admission

This nightclub is a favorite with young, energetic travelers and features the sound of live rock. You'll find plenty of activity here.

THE PLANET NITECLUB
Islander Complex, Seven Mile Beach
☎ 345/949-7169
www.planet.ky
Admission

This dance club is also a favorite with young travelers (read: beware during spring break!). Nightly activities range from Caribbean night to reggae and soca night to dance music.

SHARKEY'S NITECLUB
Cayman Falls Shopping Centre
West Bay Rd., Seven Mile Beach
☎ 345/945-5366
Admission

This nightclub is known for its dancing, with live rock and roll Tuesdays, comedy on Wednesday, Thursdays, Saturdays and Sundays (see Chuckles Comedy Club, below), and big screen music theme nights.

Piano Bar

LOGGIA LOUNGE
Hyatt Regency Grand Cayman
West Bay Rd., Seven Mile Beach
☎ 345/949-1234, ext. 5209

When you are looking for a quiet, sophisticated place to have a nightcap and some conversation, the Loggia Lounge is a good choice. The lounge has a humidor filled with Cuba's finest and a piano player tinkling out quiet favorites.

Comedy Clubs

COCONUTS COMEDY CLUB
Falls Plaza (across from the Westin), Seven Mile Beach
☎ 345/949-NUTS
Hours: 9 pm, Wed, Thur, Sat, Sun
Admission

For nearly a decade, Coconuts has been making visitors and residents laugh, first at the Holiday Inn and now at Legendz in the Falls Plaza. Comics stay one or two weeks at the club; reservations are suggested.

CHUCKLES COMEDY CLUB
☎ 345/945-5077
Hours: vary by location
Admission

This is sort of a floating comedy club, moving between the West Bay Polo Club and Sharkey's, depending on the night of the week. Several nights a week the club features the Big Kahuna.

Sports Bars

DURTY REID'S
Red Bay Plaza, George Town
☎ 345/947-1860

This sports bar says it has "warm beer, lousy food, and surly help." Have some jerk chicken or pork and judge for yourself!

CAPTAIN BRYAN'S PATIO BY THE SEA
North Church Street at Mary St., George Town
☎ 345/949-6163
Inexpensive

Order up a half-pint of Tennent's Extra or
Stone's Best Bitter at this bar that calls itself
the best British pub for 5,000 miles. Extensive
beer selection and pub grub. Pub menu includes
steak and kidney pie, cod and chips, chicken
and mushroom pie, bangers and mash, and
shepherd's pie. Out on the patio, enjoy a menu
featuring local seafood.

Captain Bryan's is noted for Irish jam sessions and dart tournaments.

LONE STAR BAR AND GRILL
West Bay Rd., Seven Mile Beach
☎ 345/945-5175

Every inch of available space seems to be occu-
pied by the donated T-shirts as well as auto-
graphed memorabilia at this bar often
patronized by visiting celebrities. The bar has
three satellites and all major games are tele-
vised. Come by for happy hour from 5-6:30 on
weekdays.

WEST BAY POLO CLUB
SPORTS BAR AND GRILL
Seven Mile Shops, West Bay Rd.
Seven Mile Beach
☎ 345/949-9892
www.poloclub.ky

More than 15 television screens (including an
80-inch screen) broadcast just about any sport-
ing event available. Pizza is served nightly
until midnight. Every night the bar also fea-

tures a special: prime rib, sushi, Tex-Mex, barbecue, pasta, or stir fry. Sunday brunch is served 10-1.

Theater

HARQUAIL THEATRE
Harquail Dr. (off West Bay Rd.)
☎ 345/949-4519 or 345/949-5477
Admission

The Harquail Theatre is operated by the Cayman National Cultural Foundation and offers several programs including theatrical presentations, a playwriting competition, Caribbean evenings, and more. Call for schedule.

West Indies Show

CARIBBEAN DINNER PARTY
Hyatt Regency Grand Cayman
West Bay Rd., Seven Mile Beach
Hours: Tuesday and Friday nights, 6:30-9:30
☎ 345/949-1234, ext. 5208
Admission

This twice-weekly show features limbo dancers, fire eaters, and a steel pan musician. The evening, which at press time was priced at CI $39, includes dinner of pepperpot soup, spicy conch stew, salads, Jamaican barbecued fish, jerk mahi mahi, and more.

Sunset & Dinner Cruises

JOLLY ROGER
Bayside Dock, George Town
☎ 345/949-8534
Admission

Sunset cruises are a popular way to see the island and a favorite with couples. On Saturdays, Sundays, Tuesdays and Thursdays this replica of a 17th-century galleon sails at dusk. Admission includes complimentary rum punch and appetizers; a full bar is also available. Cruises cost US $25 per adult, $15 for children. The *Jolly Roger* also offers dinner cruises on Monday, Wednesday, and Friday evenings for US $55 for adults. Those evenings include complimentary rum punch and appetizers, Caribbean entrées with wine, dessert and coffee. Reservations must be made by 2 pm the day of the cruise.

CAPT. BRYANS
The Buccaneer, Seven Mile Beach
☎ 345/949-0038
Admission

Sunset cruises are available on Tuesday through Saturday nights. Cash bar.

COCKATOO
Parrots Landing, George Town
☎ 345/949-7884
Admission

This sailing catamaran offers sunset sails from 5 pm to 7 pm for CI $20. Cost includes fruit punch; BYOB welcomed.

RED SAIL SPORTS
Multiple locations, including Seven Mile Beach
☎ 345/945-5965

We recently took a sunset dinner cruise with Red Sail Sports – it was one of the highlights of our trip. Red Sail Sports offers this sunset cruise from Rum Point on Sundays and other days from Seven Mile Beach. The two-hour sunset cruise departs at 5 pm, during the winter months and 5:30 during the summer. Complimentary appetizers are served; a full cash bar is available. Cost is US $27.50 for adults, half-price for children. Dinner cruises are also available with three courses; cost is $62 for adults and children under 12 half price.

Cinema

There's one movie theater in the Cayman Islands: **Cinema I & II**, located on West Bay Road along Seven Mile Beach. For features, check the *Caymanian Compass* or call ☎ 345/949-4011 or 949-2632.

Grand Cayman A-Z

American Consulate

The **US Consular Agency** on Grand Cayman is in Rankin's Plaza, Eastern Avenue, George Town.

American Express Office

The American Express Travel Service office is at Elizabethan Square on Shedden Road in George Town. For information, ☎ 345/949-8755 or 949-8351; fax 949-5602.

Babysitting

Most of the larger hotels offer babysitting services (and some, such as the Hyatt and Westin, have supervised kids' programs). Another option is **Baby Sitting and More** (☎ 345/949-1509), which offers babysitting in your room by mothers; nursing by registered nurses is also available by the licensed and insured company.

Banks

Here a bank, there a bank, everywhere a bank! With almost 600 banks on the island, you're never far from financial services. Most are found in George Town and offer all the services you'd expect at home, including ATMs.

Currency Exchange

Left with some Caymanian money upon departure? Not to worry – at the airport there's a currency exchange booth in the departure lounge at the bar. We were surprised to see rates better than the bank here!

Dentists

Cayman Dental Services (☎ 345/947-4447) has dentists on call 24 hours a day, just in case. You can also call the **Merren Dental Center** after hours (☎ 345/949-2554, emergencies ☎ 345/947-1865) or **Robert Parr, DDS** (☎ 345/949-6384, emergencies ☎ 345/947-6177).

Grocery Stores

Many condominium owners stock up on groceries and have breakfast or lunch in their rooms. The island has several supermarkets: **Kirk Supermarket** at Eastern Avenue and West Bay Road, **Foster's Food Fair** (with two locations: The Strand along West Bay Road and Airport Road), and **Hurley's Supermarket** in Eden Shopping Centre on Walkers Road in George Town. In West Bay, **Republix Supermarket** has groceries (as well as same-day film processing).

Hyperbaric Chamber

A two-person recompression chamber is available at the **George Town Hospital** on Grand

Cayman. The facility is available 24 hours daily.

Emergency Phone Numbers

For medical emergencies, ☎ 911 or 555.

Hospital

Grand Cayman is home to the **George Town Hospital**, which offers modern medical facilities; the hospital was recently renovated and expanded. Medivac facilities can be arranged at the airport when patients need to be flown to the US.

There are two medical clinics on Grand Cayman: **Professional Medical Centre** (☎ 345/949-6066) and **Cayman Medical and Surgical Centre** (☎ 345/949-8150).

Optical Services

Lose a contact lens or break your glasses? Stop by **Cayman Optical Express** (Seven Mile Shops, West Bay Rd., ☎ 345/949-9600) or **Optical Outlook** (Caymanian Village, North Sound Way, ☎ 345/949-0539).

Pharmacies

Strand Pharmacy (The Strand Shopping Centre on West Bay Road), is open 7 am-10 pm Monday through Saturday, 9 am-6 pm Sunday. **Cayman Drug** in the Kirk Freeport Center in George Town is the largest on the island.

Island Pharmacy at West Shore Centre on West Bay Road has pharmaceutical products as well as small gifts, suntan lotions, and more.

Photo Labs

With the huge dive business encouraging a lot of underwater photography, you'll find great photo service on island, including one-hour processing services. Some excellent labs include:

- ❖ **Cayman Camera:** downtown across from the *Atlantis* Submarine office. ☎ 345/949-8359.

- ❖ **Hottrax Photo:** West Shore Center, Seven Mile Beach. ☎ 345/949-9047.

- ❖ **Photo Center:** Waterfront, George Town. ☎ 345/949-0030.

- ❖ **Photo Plus:** Photo Pharm Centre, Smith Road, George Town. ☎ 345/949-2420.

Post Office

Postage from the Cayman Islands to the US is CI 20¢ for a postcard, CI 30¢ for letters weighing up to a half-ounce.

Grand Cayman has no postal delivery routes, so all mail is placed in the boxes of either the Main post office in George Town or the Westhore Branch on West Bay Road.

The main post office serves as home for the **philatelic bureau**, open 8:30 to 5:30 Monday through Friday, and 8:30 to 1 on Saturday for Caymanian stamps and first-day covers.

Religious Services

Bahai, Boggy Sand Rd., West Bay, ☎ 345/949-3435.

Catholic, St. Ignatius, Walker's Rd., George Town, ☎ 345/949-6797; Christ the Redeemer Mission, West Bay.

Church of England, South Sound Community Centre, ☎ 345/949-2757.

Church of God, Walker's Rd., George Town, ☎ 345/949-9395.

Church of Jesus Christ (LDS), Smith Rd., ☎ 345/949-4499.

Elmslie United Church (Presbyterian), Harbour Dr., George Town, ☎ 345/949-7923.

First Baptist Church, Smith Rd., George Town, ☎ 345/949-0692.

Seventh Day Adventists, Creme Rd., George Town, ☎ 345/947-5279.

St. George Anglican Church, George Town Cts. off Eastern Ave., George Town, ☎ 345/949-5583.

Wesleyan Holiness Church, Turtle Farm Rd., West Bay, ☎ 345/949-3394.

Room Tax

A 10% government tax is charged on all accommodations. Most hotels add gratuities ranging from 6-10% to this amount.

Shoe Repair

If you bust a sole during your visit, stop by **No. 1 Shoe Repair**, Jetik Building, Walkers Road in George Town (☎ 345/949-5595).

Spas

Recently the Hyatt Regency resort opened Grand Cayman's first full-service spa. The **Britannia Beauty Spa**, a two-story, 1,980-square-foot facility, is staffed by European-trained therapists. It offers several wet and dry treatment rooms, relaxation room, and juice bar, hydrotherapy tub, steam shower cabin, and a new pool. Guests can select from numerous treatments, including reflexology, seaweed treatments, aromatherapy facials and massage, skin brushing, body exfoliating, Swedish massage, hydrotherapy and more.

Telephone Service

The Cayman Islands have excellent telecommunications service thanks to Cable & Wireless (Cayman Islands) Ltd. You'll find dependable, modern phone and internet service on each of the islands.

The area code for the Cayman Islands is 345.

AT&T, MCI Direct and **US Sprint** services are available for dialing from the islands to home.

For information on telephone charges, see page 38.

Throughout the islands, you'll find many public phones. Some accept coins only; others accept phone cards only; some accept both. You can purchase phone cards in denominations of $10, $15 and $25 at the Cable and Wireless office on Anderson Square on Shedden Road in George Town, at the Cayman Brac office and at most service stations.

Video Rentals

Because of all the condominium properties with VCRs, you'll find a good selection of rental businesses on Grand Cayman. **Blockbuster** has locations at the Eden Centre in George Town (☎ 345/949-9500) and on West Bay Road in the **Westshore Centre** (☎ 345/949-4500).

Website

Check out the Cayman Islands Department of Tourism Website at www.caymanislands.ky for news and weather as well as details on accommodations, attractions, and more. You can also order brochures or send questions to the Department of Tourism through an e-mail link from the site.

Little Cayman

Just 80 miles northeast of Grand Cayman but worlds apart in terms of atmosphere, Little Cayman is tailor-made for visitors looking for secluded scuba diving, fly or spin fishing, and nature. Appropriate to its name, Little Cayman spans only 11 miles in length and two miles at its widest point. Boasting none of the glitz of Grand Cayman, Little Cayman does greet guests with all the basic comforts, including several small lodges and condominiums with air-conditioning, satellite television, and telephone service.

With just over 100 permanent residents, the island's largest population is that of birds and iguanas. Over 2,000 Little Cayman Rock Iguanas inhabit the island, so many that "Iguana Crossing" and "Iguana Right of Way" signs are posted throughout the island to protect these lizards, which can grow up to five feet in length.

Little Cayman's chief draw is its ecotourism: diving, fishing, and bird watching. The late Philipe Cousteau called the island's Bloody Bay Wall one of the best dives of his life; today it's still a favorite with divers.

Anglers come to this tiny isle for its excellent bonefishing. Bonefish and permit, both caught in the flats, and tarpon, reeled in from brackish

Tarpon Lake, draw fishermen. The Southern Cross Club fishing lodge first attracted anglers to these waters; today McCoy's Diving and Fishing Lodge also caters to fishermen. Guests at other island resorts can arrange fishing guides from these lodges.

Birders enjoy the Booby Pond Visitors Centre. Operated by the National Trust, this 1.2-acre brackish mangrove pond is the home of the Caribbean's largest breeding colony of red-footed boobies and a breeding colony of magnificent frigate birds. Visitors can view the birds from two telescopes (available for use any time) and see exhibits on the birds of Little Cayman in the visitors center. Admission is free although donations are welcomed.

Getting There

The dirt airstrip of **Edward Bodden Airport** has twice-daily service from Grand Cayman. **Island Air** (☎ 800/9-CAYMAN or 345/949-5252, Monday through Sunday 9 am to 5 pm) departs on the 45-minute flight at 8 am and 3:50 pm; return flights depart at 9:55 am and 5:45 pm. Round-trip tickets are US $122 (US $98 for passengers under 12); a day trip package is also available for US $105 (US $84 for travelers under 12).

Passengers may check up to 55 pounds of baggage free of charge; excess baggage is charged

US 50¢ per pound. Service is also available from Little Cayman to Cayman Brac twice daily.

Day Trips From Grand Cayman

Island Air offers three packages for visiting Little Cayman if you're staying on Grand Cayman. Visit as a day traveler for US $159, including air, lunch, and sightseeing. If you'd like to spend one night on the island, take the Little Cayman Adventure II package for US $236 including air, sightseeing tour, and accommodations at the Little Cayman Beach Resort. A two-night trip is available for $309.

Getting Around

Car & Jeep Rental

Only one rental car agency operates on the island. **McLaughlin Jeep Rental** (☎ 345/948-1000, fax 345/948-1001) offers daily and weekly rates for jeeps; only standard transmission jeeps are available. To call the rental agency on arrival, visitors pick up the phone located on the side of the airport building. Vehicles are left drive; driving is on the left side of the road. Rates start at US $59 daily.

Driver's Permits

There is a 25 mph speed limit on the island.

A Caymanian driver's permit is required for rentals; obtain one at McLaughlin's for a US $7.50 fee. A major credit card or cash deposit is also required.

Bicycles

Another popular mode of transportation is the bicycle. Guests will find that most resorts offer complimentary use of bicycles and, with practically no traffic on the roads, they offer a peaceful way to see the island, journey to a secluded beach, or pop into Blossom Village. The old cycles may not be the fastest vehicles, but, after all, this is Little Cayman. What's the hurry?

Orientation

Blossom Village

Most of the island's residents live on its southernmost tip near a community called Blossom Village. Here's you'll find island services, including the airport, car rental agency, grocery store, gas station, real estate office, restaurant, and several accommodations. The island's main road carves through town, but there's certainly no need to worry about traffic.

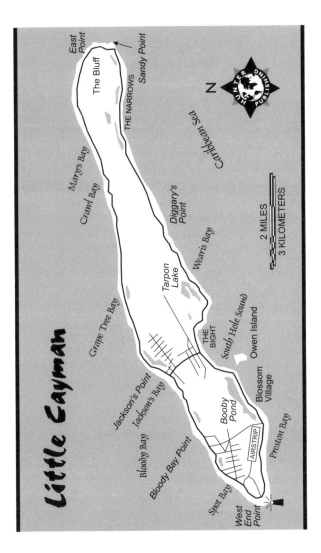

Little Cayman

So little happens on this island, in fact, that there's only one policeman (but locals warn that he's happy to use his new radar speed gun) and one taxi (but the driver has another job, so don't expect pick up at a moment's notice).

Past the main road, side streets wind through Blossom Village, curving past cheery neighborhoods where everyone knows one another and visitors are greeted with waves and smiles. A small cemetery, many of its graves marked with conch shells and white crosses bleached even whiter by the Caribbean sun, marks the final resting place of former Little Cayman residents.

Parallel to Blossom Village stretches a protected marine park, home of some of the top snorkeling and dive spots on the island. Here divers find Grundy Gardens, Windsock, Harlod's Holes, Jay's Reef, Charlie's Chimney's, Patty's Point, Pirates Reef and Preston Reef, each the location of myriad marine life and underwater formations. Several dive operators offer trips to popular sites.

Beyond Blossom Village

Beyond Blossom Village, the main road, known formally as Guy Banks Road on the southern stretch of the island, winds north past scrubby brushland. Soon the road passes the Booby **Pond Nature Reserve**, a brackish mangrove pond. Trees are dotted with white birds – red-footed boobies – and overhead the distinct shape of the magnificent frigate bird can be seen soaring on the trade winds.

The bay to the north of Owen Island is known as **South Hole Sound** and this inlet marks one of the few intersections on the island. Here the Crossover Road, or more formally Spot Bay Road, crosses to the other side of the island.

Continuing north, the main road soon loses its pavement and gives way to packed dirt and sand, safe for all vehicles. Stay on the road, however, because deep sand is found at some turnoffs. Along this stretch of road you'll pass many shallow ponds on the left side, each lined with low vegetation that forms a home for the island's bountiful bird population. Birders enjoy a drive by **Tarpon Lake**, a brackish lake filled with tarpon. A favorite with anglers, the lake has tarpon ranging from three to 15 pounds. Birders will find more interest along the pond's shoreline.

Scrubby undergrowth grows thick as you work your way to the north side of the island, climbing a slight rise. This is the island's driest end, a place where the terrain becomes marked with tall cacti and century plants (agave).

East Point is the easternmost point of the island. From here you can see nearby Cayman Brac, located seven miles across the channel. This stretch of Little Cayman is nearly deserted, with just a few lone cacti overlooking acres of undeveloped land.

The road then turns back south and traces the northern coast of Little Cayman, a stretch that's one of the favorites with divers. By far the most popular area is **Bloody Bay Wall**, located near where the Crossover Road comes out on the north coast road. This stretch of coastline is a marine park, safeguarding what has often been called one of the best dive locations on the globe.

★ DID YOU KNOW?

For many years, Little Cayman's most famous resident, actor Burgess Meredith, had a vacation home along this coastline.

Best Places to Stay

Alive Price Scale - Accommodations

Deluxe . . . . $300+
Expensive . . . . $200-$300
Moderate . . . . $100-$200
Inexpensive . . . . Under $100

Resorts & Hotels

LITTLE CAYMAN BEACH RESORT

PO Box 51, Blossom Village
Little Cayman, BWI
☎ 813/323-8727, fax 813/323-8827
Reservations: ☎ 800/ 327-3835
www.littlecayman.com
Moderate

Little Cayman Beach Resort brings together the amenities of a Grand Cayman resort with the privacy of a getaway on Little Cayman. The island's largest property is specially tailored for those who want luxury intermingled with adventures. This pink, two-story conch-shell pink resort overlooks a shallow area inside the reef on the south side of the island. Just outside the reef lie top scuba spots accessible through Reef Divers, the on-site operator. Beginners can learn with a resort course or obtain open water certification.

Underwater photographers can see their shots the same day; an underwater photo and video center has E-6 processing and rentals.

Non-divers also enjoy this resort for its laid-back atmosphere. Hammocks sway just yards from the shoreline; loungers line the edge of the freshwater pool a few steps from the bar.

Rooms include air-conditioning, balcony or patio, color TV, ceiling fan, and beach. New oceanfront rooms include wetbars, microwaves and coffeemakers. There's a bar, gift shop, restaurant, freshwater pool, dive shop, underwater photo center, fitness center and hot tub.

PIRATES POINT RESORT
Box 43, Preston Bay
Little Cayman, BWI
☎ 345/948-1010, fax 345/948-1011
Moderate

This 12-room resort is a favorite with divers and it's easy to see why. Four dive instructors reveal the secrets of Bloody Bay Wall, from sheer cliffs to delicate sponges and coral formations.

Non-divers find plenty of activity (or non-activity, if they so choose) at Pirates Point as well. Owner Gladys Howard is active in eco-tourism. The lobby of Pirates Point is filled with nature guidebooks, and Gladys also has a nature trail guide and fishing guide to take visitors out for a day or half-day of fishing, birding, or just to learn more about the island's indigenous species.

The resort offers plenty of temptation to just laze the day away on a powdery white beach as well. Guest cottages are simple and light, decorated in Caribbean colors. Rooms include ceiling fan, tile floors, and private baths. Drinking water is produced by the resort's own reverse-osmosis plant.

After a day in the sun, guests can relax in the island's unique bar, furnished with artwork created by previous guests. (The grounds of Pirates Point also feature guest-donated artwork, made of everything from coconut shells to driftwood.)

But there's no doubt that dining ranks as one of the top attractions at Pirates Point. Along with her expertise in natural history, Gladys Howard is also a cordon bleu chef. While guests may like roughing it during the day, at night they can enjoy gourmet meals as elegant as those found at any of the Caribbean's finest resorts. Gladys boasts that "my kitchen never closes."

An all-inclusive dive package is available, including a deluxe room with private bath, three gourmet meals daily (with wine), open bar with unlimited drinks, two boat dives daily, use of all dive equipment, airport transfers, use of bicycles, and hammocks, lounges, and beach towels. And for non-divers, an all-inclusive package includes everything except diving. Hotel tax and 15% gratuity are not included.

SAM McCOY'S DIVE LODGE
PO Box 29
Little Cayman, BWI
☎ 345/948-0026, fax 345/948-0057
Reservations: ☎ 800/626-0496
Moderate

One of the island's earliest accommodations remains a favorite, especially with divers and fishermen. Two dive boats, the 30-foot *Caymaniac* and the 28-foot *Caymanak*, transport divers to sites around the island. Anglers can head out aboard the 32-foot *Reel McCoy* deep-sea fishing boat.

Eight guest rooms greet visitors with rustic charm. Tucked beneath shady trees and always in sight of the deserted beach, the rooms feature private baths, air-conditioning, and guests can dine right on premises. Other facilities include a small freshwater pool with Jacuzzi jets.

Grill up the day's catch on BBQs provided at this resort.

SOUTHERN CROSS CLUB
PO Box 44
Little Cayman, BWI
☎ 345/948-1099, fax 345/948-1098
Reservations: ☎ 800/899-2582
Moderate

The Southern Cross holds the distinction as the island's first resort. Located along South Hole Sound, this resort was recently renovated. Today five beachfront cottages offer 10 guest rooms decorated in island colors; each room has air-conditioning, ceiling fans, (no phones or TV) and plenty of water from the inn's own desalinization plant. Facilities include a freshwater swimming pool and outdoor bar.

Southern Cross has long been a favorite destination with Caribbean anglers. Both deep-sea and tackle fishing for bonefish, tarpon, and permit are offered here. The Southern Cross Club has a 24-foot deep-sea fishing boat and a resident fishing guide to make sure you'll return home with plenty of fish tales.

Divers also find everything they need at this resort. Three dive boats offer daily dives at this PADI and NAUI certified shop. This is now an IANTD Nitrox facility.

If a day of diving and fishing builds your appetites, that's no problem at this resort. One of the managers, Stephanie Shaw, is trained by the Culinary Institute of America and she oversees meals for both guests and day visitors alike.

Condominiums

CONCH CLUB CONDOMINIUMS
PO Box 51, Blossom Village
Little Cayman, BWI
☎ 813/323-8727
Reservations: ☎ 800/327-3835
www.conchclub.com
Deluxe

Located just north of Blossom Village, this upscale condominium project is an exciting development on Little Cayman. The resort offers a host of amenities: a restaurant, bar, fitness center, game room, beauty shop, and more. The lemon-yellow units are excellent for several couples traveling together or for families. Divers will find the Conch Club in walking distance of one of the island's best dive shops. The two-story condominiums are just steps from the powdery beach.

The property has been undergoing expansion. Phase two was underway at press time with eight two- and three-bedroom units with ceramic tile floors, carpeted bedrooms, ceiling fans, central air-conditioning, washer and dryer and more. The new addition joins the 12 units in phase one.

The complex now offers two- and three-bedroom units. Two-bedroom units, spanning 1,700 square feet, include one queen, two twins, and one double convertible bed as well as 2½ baths. At 2,000 square feet, the three-bedroom units offer one queen, one double, and two twin beds, plus three baths. All units have a fully equipped kitchen, living and dining room, laundry facilities, ceiling fans, daily housekeeping, and use of pool, Jacuzzi, and dock on the property.

Several meal plans are available for guests. Meals are taken at the Bird of Paradise Restaurant at Little Cayman Beach Resort, located next door.

Guests at the Conch Club can also enjoy scuba diving next door at Little Cayman Beach Resort. Full equipment rental, diving courses, and underwater photography equipment is available.

Villas

PARADISE VILLAS
PO Box 48
Little Cayman, BWI
☎ 345/948-0001, fax 345/948-0002
Moderate

Located next door to the Hungry Iguana restaurant (and just steps from Blossom Village), these cozy villas are perfect for those who'd like housekeeping facilities but the option of both a nearby eatery and a grocery store. These villas, two units to a cottage, lie right on the beach. Each includes two twin beds or one king, a futon that can sleep one adult or two kids, a back patio overlooking the sea, full kitchen with microwave, toaster and coffee maker, and air-conditioning. Facilities include a swimming pool and nearby restaurant.

SEA VIEW VILLA
PO Box 29
Little Cayman, BWI
Reservations: ☎ 317/846-7017, fax 317/846-0217
Expensive

This villa rents by the week and can accommodate up to six guests in its two bedrooms. Located on the island's south side, it has air-conditioning, ceiling fans, telephones, television and more.

CAYMAN VILLAS
Reservations: ☎ 800/235-5888
www.caymanvillas.com

Cayman Villas represents several properties on Little Cayman in a variety of price ranges:

SUNSET COTTAGE
Deluxe

This two-bedroom, two-bath home is located seaside. It includes a screened porch off the master bedroom and another off the living/guest bedroom.

SUZY'S COTTAGE
Expensive

This one-bedroom property on a white sand beach can host up to six guests. Amenities include air-conditioning, ceiling fans, telephones, television, and more.

LITTLE CAYMAN COTTAGE
Expensive

This two-bedroom cottage is situated on the beach and can accommodate up to six guests. The cottage has a screened porch but is not air-conditioned.

Small Hotels/Live-Aboards

LITTLE CAYMAN DIVER II
☎ 800/458-BRAC
Deluxe

Well, it's not exactly a small inn, but this live-aboard operates much like one. Based off Little Cayman, the boat accommodates 10 passengers in five cabins, each with a private bath. PADI, NAUI, SSI, NASDS, and YMCA affiliated, this operator has been in business for 10 years. Video rentals offered.

Best Places to Eat

Money Matters

Visa, Mastercard, American Express, Diners Club, and Access are commonly accepted; Discover is accepted at some establishments.

Some restaurants add a 15% gratuity to the bill, so make sure you don't inadvertently tip twice.

Alive Price Scale - Restaurants

Expensive . . . . $40+
Moderate . . . . $25-$40
Inexpensive . . . . Under $25

Informal Dining

The only stand-alone restaurant on the island is the **Hungry Iguana**, located near the airport. The seaside eatery, named for an iguana often seen at the airport, now sports a 40-foot mural of its namesake. Continental buffet breakfasts start the day; lunch and dinner feature jerk chicken, grouper sandwiches, prime rib, and burgers. ☎ 345/948-0007.

Resort Restaurants

A surprising number of resorts also feature top-notch dining. **Pirates Point** (☎ 345/948-1010) showcases the talents of cordon bleu owner-chef Gladys Howard and serves up gourmet cuisine; the **Southern Cross Club** (☎ 800/899-2582) features a Culinary Institute of America-trained chef.

Dawn to Dusk

Beaches

All beaches in the Cayman Islands are public.

Owen Island

Owen Island, seen to the right as you travel north from Blossom Village, is an uninhabited island. It spans just 11 acres and is a popular day trip destination for picnickers, who can reach the island's sandy beaches by row boat.

Sandy Point

Swimmers and picnickers find an excellent spot at Point of Sand, a.k.a. Sandy Point. Turn right off the main road. The turn is easy to find: it's the only turn where the interacting road sports a stop sign. The sand is packed for the first half of the drive; stop at the wide section where it's powdery.

Do not attempt to take vehicles down to the beach; the sand is too deep.

❊ TIP

It's a long walk back to town and there are no facilities or telephones in this park.

This beach, luminescent with beautiful pink sand, is one of the island's prettiest and also most secluded. You very well might spend the entire day on this stretch of beach and never see another person. On weekends visitors from Cayman Brac often visit here. A covered picnic table invites you to enjoy a quiet lunch with the sound of the sea as background music.

Scuba Diving

Its name may be "little," but this island is a giant in the world of scuba diving. Along its 10-mile length, 57 dive sites are marked with moorings. The most famous site is Bloody Bay Wall on the

north side of the island. The wall drops off just a short swim from the shore at a depth of only 20 feet, making it a favorite with snorkelers as well. See page 220 for a list of dive operators.

Molly the Manta

Divers who have enjoyed Little Cayman for
many years will miss Molly the Manta, a giant manta ray once often seen on night
dives in this region. With a 12-foot span, the
manta was spotted along the north coast
and on the south coast flats from 1991
through 1995. She was also seen off Bloody
Bay and would swoop through the water,
scooping up plankton that were attracted by
divers' lights. Today Molly is no longer
around, and it is believed she has reached
maturity and gone off in search of a mate.

Best Dive Sites

Bloody Bay Wall

Starting at a depth of just 25 feet, this site is a
favorite with every level of diver and is considered one of the best dive sites in the Caribbean.
Named one of the top dive sites by the late
Philipe Cousteau, the wall is thick with
sponges and corals and also features many formations such as chimneys, canyons, and coral
arches. The wall is a spectacular sight, dropping into sheer blackness from, just inches
away, the clear turquoise shallows.

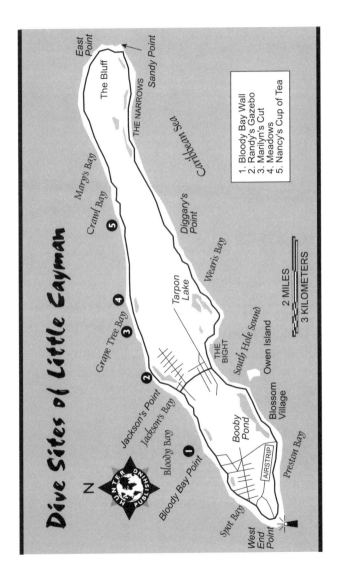

Dive Sites of Little Cayman

N

HUNTER PUBLISHING

1. Bloody Bay Wall
2. Randy's Gazebo
3. Marilyn's Cut
4. Meadows
5. Nancy's Cup of Tea

2 MILES

3 KILOMETERS

East Point
The Bluff
Sandy Point
THE NARROWS
Mary's Bay
Crawl Bay
Caribbean Sea
Diggary's Point
Wear's Bay
Grape Tree Bay
Tarpon Lake
Jackson's Point
Jackson's Bay
THE BIGHT
South Hole Sound
Owen Island
Blossom Village
Bloody Bay
Bloody Bay Point
Booby Pond
AIRSTRIP
Preston Bay
Spot Bay
West End Point

Nancy's Cup of Tea

On the north side of the island off Big Channel, this dive site begins at a depth of just 35 feet before plunging into inky waters. Decorated with multicolored sponges as well as gorgonians. Look for lots of marine life here.

Meadows

West of Nancy's Cup of Tea, this shallow site is home to eagle rays, groupers, and more. Small caverns and overhangs make this spot special.

Marilyn's Cut

This site is also home to a favorite resident: Ben, a Nassau grouper.

Off Grape Tree Bay on the north side of the island, the cut or crevice leads to a wall filled with sponges and gorgonians.

Randy's Gazebo

Out from Jackson's Point, Randy's Gazebo is noted for its tunnels and swim-throughs. This wall dive includes a natural arch that's a favorite with underwater photographers.

Dive & Snorkel Operators

All phone numbers listed here are area code 345, unless indicated otherwise.

Paradise Divers	☎ 948-0001
Pirates Point Resort	☎ 948-1010
Reef Divers (Little Cayman Beach Resort)	☎ 800/327-3835

Sam McCoy's	☎ 948-0026 or 800/626-0496
Diving and Fishing Lodge	
Southern	☎ 948-1099 or 800/899-2582
Cross Club	

Snorkel Excursions

Several operators offer snorkel trips to some of the island's shallower sites, including Bloody Bay Wall. Snorkel trips run between $15 and $35.

Fishing

Shore, reef, and deep-sea fishing are available year around and local guides can provide tackle and point out the best fishing spots. Catch-and-release is encouraged by local captains and applies to all catches that will be not eaten and all billfish that aren't record contenders.

Reef fishing is also found along the many miles of reefs that surround this island.

Little Cayman is the top destination of the three Cayman Islands for those using light tackle and fly fishing.

Fly fishing continues to grow in popularity here but anglers should bring all their equipment – guides and charters do not supply saltwater fly rods.

Bonefishing, while not as good as some islands in the Caribbean or the Florida Keys, is a favorite activity and a challenge to anglers.

These three- to eight-pound fish are seen in the shallow areas called muds, places where the sea is churned up by the bottom-feeding fish.

Guides recommend baiting with fry. Bonefish can be caught all day although, like other types of fishing, the success rate depends on many factors such as weather and tides. The best bonefishing around Little Cayman is usually found at the **South Hole Sound**.

Tarpon fishing is also popular on Little Cayman. Tarpon Pond, a brackish lake north of Blossom Village, is home to many 20 pound tarpon. Fly fishermen will have best luck at this site in early morning and late afternoon.

If you are looking for deep water action, charters seek gamefish, including blue marlin, yellowfin tuna, wahoo, dolphin (dorado) and barracuda. Taking out a charter boat is not an inexpensive proposition, but for many visitors it's the highlight of their trip. A half-day charter begins at about US $400 and may range as high as $1,000 for a full-day trip aboard a large charter with state-of-the art equipment and tackle.

Fishing Guides

Whether you're staying on the island or coming over on a day trip, you can enjoy fishing with a local guide if you give advance notice.

SAM McCOY'S FISHING & DIVING LODGE
☎ 800/626-0496, 345/948-0026

McCoy's Lodge has guides on staff year-round. Sam McCoy has been leading fishing excursions on this island for 30 years and son Chip McCoy is widely considered the best light tackle fishing guide on the island (he also offers fly fishing). Fishermen should bring their own fly fishing equipment, but light tackle equipment is available. McCoy's is also fully equipped for deep-sea fishing; ice, bait, and tackle are provided.

SOUTHERN CROSS CLUB
☎ 345/948-1099

Three vessels, 16 to 24 feet, take groups of two, three or four deep-sea fishing. Full- and half-day reef fishing also available.

Unique Tours

Guided Tours

Guided tours of the island are led by Gladys Howard, National Trust Chapter Chairman and owner of the Pirates Point Resort. They are conducted every Sunday morning; for more information contact the **Cayman Islands National Trust**, ☎ 345/949-0121, or **Gladys Howard**, ☎ 345/948-1010. A CI $1 donation to the Little Cayman National Trust is requested.

Self-Guided Hikes

Little Cayman presents travelers with plenty of walking and hiking opportunities. Almost non-existent traffic, a flat grade on all but the island's easternmost end, and wide roads make Little Cayman perfect for a stroll or hike. Stroll the quiet streets of Blossom Village, the main road out to Tarpon Lake, or the island's beautiful beaches.

Island Sightseeing

Most of the sights on Little Cayman are natural rather than man-made. Outdoor activities, especially scuba diving and fishing, draw most visitors.

Bruce's Turtle Nursery

For a look at Cayman's local turtles, stop by Bruce's Turtle Nursery. It's not the Cayman Turtle Farm, but that's part of its charm – just park your car and follow the ropes back to the turtle tanks for a self-guided, free look at these marine creatures. Three tanks hold green sea turtles. The nursery is next to Bluewater Divers in Blossom Village.

Booby Pond Visitors Centre

Birders enjoy this facility, open Monday through Saturday, 2-5 pm. Operated by the National Trust, this 1.2-mile-long brackish mangrove pond is the home of the Caribbean's largest breeding colony of red-footed boobies (*Sula Sula*) and a breeding colony of magnificent frigate birds. Approximately 30% of the Caribbean population of red-footed boobies resides at this pond. Even without the help of binoculars, you can view the large white birds (or their large, gray offspring) in the trees. Over 7,000 make their home here. The Visitors Centre includes exhibits on the island's many indigenous species, from the common crab to the seed shrimp to the pond's many resident birds. Friendly volunteers staff the center and welcome questions about the wildlife and about island life.

★ DID YOU KNOW?

The visitors center is part of the Booby Pond Nature Reserve which has been designated an international RAMSAR site. For this recognition, which falls under the United Nations convention to protect wetlands for waterfowl habitats, a site must meet strict environmental criteria and be protected by local law.

For a close-up look you can view the birds from two telescopes (available for use any time) on the porch. One telescope is positioned for use with wheelchairs or for those who would like to sit. The boobies fly about 40 mph and nest in crude constructions made of rough sticks. Admission is free, although donations are welcomed. A small gift shop sells locally made crafts and artwork.

What's That Rotten Egg Smell?

Occasionally, Booby Pond will smell like rotten eggs or sulfur. The odor is the result of hydrogen sulfide gas created from decomposing organic material in the pond. Under normal conditions, the gas is released into the pond water, but when the water level drops the harmless gas is released into the air.

Shop Til You Drop

 Little Cayman is not a shopper's paradise. Don't look for duty-free bargains or anything resembling a good selection of merchandise.

Resort Stores

What you will find are assorted small gift stores around the island, primarily at the resorts. At

Little Cayman Beach Resort, **Mermaids** sells jewelry, Spanish coins, clothes, and gift items; the shop is open afternoons only, Monday through Saturday. T-shirts and some souvenir items can be found at the grocery store and the small shop adjoining McLaughlin's rental agency in **Blossom Village**. A small gift shop at **Pirates Point** sells a variety of items, including a Little Cayman cookbook prepared by Gladys Howard for the National Trust.

Traveling With Children

Families will find that cribs are available at most properties. However, bring baby needs, including disposable diapers and baby food. They're difficult to find on Little Cayman.

After Dark

Vacationers don't come to Little Cayman for the nightlife. Most simply rest up in preparation for the next day's dive. The best way to spend an evening is to enjoy a relaxing meal at one of the resorts, then go for a walk on the beach. Moonlit strolls through Blossom Village also make a good end to the day.

Little Cayman A-Z

Banks

Cayman National Bank has a branch on Little Cayman in Blossom Village on Guy Banks Rd., ☎ 345/948-0051.

Emergency Phone Numbers

For medical emergencies, ☎ 911 or 555.

Photo Lab

There is a photo center at **Little Cayman Beach Resort**. It offers rentals, film, and processing.

Room Tax

A 10% government tax is charged on all accommodations. Most hotels add gratuities ranging from 6-10% to this amount.

Telephone

The area code for Little Cayman is 345. Like Grand Cayman, Little Cayman also has service from AT&T, MCI Direct and US Sprint.

Calls within Little Cayman are charged a flat fee of 9¢ per minute. Calls between Little Cayman and Grand Cayman are 3¢ per minute. Calls between Little Cayman and Cayman Brac are 9¢ per minute.

Website

Check out news and accommodations on the Sister Islands at the Department of Tourism's official Website: www.caymanislands.ky.

Cayman Brac

If Grand Cayman is the flashy big brother of the Cayman Islands, swelled with pride in its lavish condominiums, full-service resorts, international dining, and top-notch diving, while Little Cayman is the family's youngest sibling, favored for its petite size and almost shy demeanor, then Cayman Brac is the middle child.

This middle sibling, however, is far from overlooked. Cayman Brac has its own special qualities, assets that include world-class diving along undersea walls, hiking in the most rugged terrain found in the Cayman Islands, caves that tempt exploration, birding, and much more.

The island is named for the "brac," Gaelic for bluff, which "soars" 140 feet up from the sea on the island's east end. It's the most distinct feature of this 12-mile-long, one-mile-wide island situated 89 miles east-northeast of Grand Cayman and just five miles from Little Cayman.

With a population of only 1,300 residents, Cayman Brac is closer in pace to Little Cayman than its big brother, Grand Cayman. Residents, or Brackers, are known for their personable nature and welcome vacationers to their sunny isle.

Getting There

Direct flights to **Cayman Brac Gerrard Smith Airport** are available from Miami, Tampa, Atlanta and Houston or from Grand Cayman aboard **Cayman Airways** (☎ 800/422-9626, from Canada ☎ 800/441-3003).

Twice-daily service from Grand Cayman is also provided on small prop planes with **Island Air** (☎ 345/949-5252, Monday through Friday 9 am to 5 pm, fax 345/949-7044). The flight takes one hour and 10 minutes, making a brief stop in Little Cayman.

Passengers may check up to 55 pounds of baggage free of charge; excess baggage is charged US 50¢ per pound.

Flights are also available on Island Air from Cayman Brac to Little Cayman and cost about US $40, round trip. Special fares are offered for children under age 12.

Getting Around

Car & Jeep Rentals

On Cayman Brac, it's a good idea to make car reservations before your trip if possible. The number of rental cars is limited.

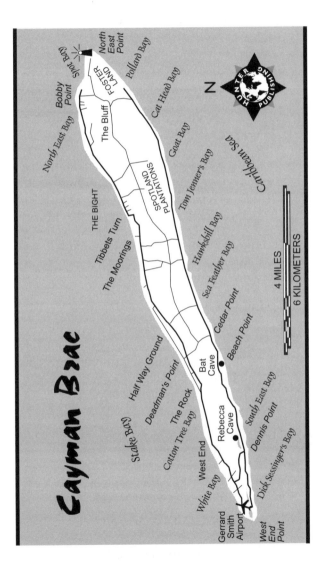

Car Rental Agencies

Brac-Rent-A-Car	☎ 345/948-1446
Brac-Hertz Rent-a-Car	☎ 345/948-1515
Four D's Car Rental	☎ 345/948-1599
T&D (Avis) Auto Rental	☎ 345/948-2424

Orientation

You won't have difficulty exploring Cayman Brac on your own – that's half the fun! You can obtain a good road map from the Department of Tourism at the airport or from your car rental agency. If you get lost, just pull over and ask a local resident for directions.

West End

Cayman Brac is a long, eel-shaped island that starts with the **Gerrard Smith Airport** on its westernmost end near a town named, appropriately enough, **West End**. This end of the island is also home to most guest accommodations and the island's only beaches.

Beyond West End

Two roads etch the perimeters of the island. **A6** traces the northern coast, starting at West End and working past Knob Hill, Banksville, Half Way Ground, Molusca Heights, Tibbetts Turn, and Spot Bay. Along the way, the road looks out on a sea that disguises several good dive sites beneath its placid waters.

On the southern shore, a road called **A7** traces its way from West End Point all the way northeast, journeying past the island's resorts, Brac Reef Beach Resort and Divi Tiara Beach Resort, past several good caves that are favorites with outdoor adventurers, and up to Pollard Bay.

A small road works through the center of the island, and this is the route to Cayman Brac's best-known attraction: the bluffs or the Brac.

Best Places to Stay

Alive Price Scale - Accommodations

Deluxe	$300+
Expensive	$200-$300
Moderate	$100-$200
Inexpensive	Under $100

Resorts & Condominiums

BRAC CARIBBEAN BEACH VILLAGE
Stake Bay
☎ 345/948-2265, fax 345/948-1111
Reservations: ☎ 800/791-7911
Moderate

This 16-room resort at Stake Bay offers air-conditioning, ceiling fans, telephones, televisions, as well as restaurant, bar, scuba, a dive shop, snorkeling, and tennis.

BRAC REEF BEACH RESORT
West End
☎ 813/323-8727
Reservations: ☎ 800/327-3835
www.braclittle.com
Moderate

This 40-room property is located off Channel Bay on the island's southeast shore. Guest rooms have air-conditioning, ceiling fans, telephones, televisions, and porches or patios. The resort also includes a pool, Jacuzzi, restaurant, bar, scuba, dive shop, snorkeling, fishing, tennis, underwater photo center and gift shop.

DIVI TIARA BEACH RESORT
Stake Bay
☎ 345/948-1553, fax 345/948-1316
Reservations: ☎ 800/367-3484
www.diviresorts.com
Moderate

Cayman Brac's largest resort offers 71 guest rooms, both standard and deluxe. Guest rooms have air-conditioning, ceiling fans, telephones, televisions, and porches or patios. The resort also includes a pool, Jacuzzi, restaurant, bar, scuba, dive shop, snorkeling, fishing, tennis, underwater photo center and gift shop.

Villas

ALMOND BEACH HIDEAWAYS
Spot Bay
☎ 541/426-4863
Reservations: ☎ 800/972-9795
www.almondbeach.com
Moderate

These three villa accommodations are some of the newest on Cayman Brac. Each two- or three-bedroom unit houses between six and eight people. These beachfront accommodations offer air-conditioning, ceiling fans, telephones, television, VCRs, kitchens, laundry facilities, barbecue grills, and more. Guest facilities include snorkeling, scuba diving, and fishing.

Guests can also opt for a dive and car rental package.

REEFSIDE RETREAT
Stake Bay
Reservations: ☎ 800/235-5888 (Cayman Villas)
www.caymanvillas.com
Moderate to Expensive

This cottage is situated right on a beach (albeit a pebble-strewn one) and offers lots of privacy. Up to four people can stay in the one-bedroom cottage. It has air-conditioning, ceiling fans, telephones, television, kitchen, laundry facilities, maid service, and more.

Guest Houses

WALTON'S MANGO MANOR
Stake Bay
☎ 345/948-0518, phone and fax
e-mail: waltons@candw.ky
Inexpensive

Cayman Brac's first bed and breakfast is within walking distance of the Cayman Brac Museum and the community of Stake Bay and is only minutes from snorkeling and shore diving. The Walton's is housed in an historic Caymanian house that formerly operated as a retirement home for Bracker seamen. Today it's a five-room guest house; rooms include air-conditioning, ceiling fans, telephones, television, and a private bath. A full breakfast is served daily.

Cayman Brac's parrots are sometimes spotted here.

This B&B is a favorite with nature lovers. It is named for a large mango tree in the front yard. You'll also see guinep, breadfuit, buttonwood and poinciana trees.

Guests have use of a barbecue and patio as well as the microwave; rental bicycles are also available.

Best Places to Eat

Restaurants on Cayman Brac tend to be casual and feature local catches – and they're inexpensive to boot.

West End

On the West End, choices include **Aunt Sha's Kitchen** for Caymanian and American dishes (☎ 345/948-1581), **Edd's Place**, serving Caymanian, American and Chinese food (☎ 345/948-1208), and the **G&M Diner** (☎ 345/948-1272) for American dishes and more.

Stake Bay

At Stake Bay, **La Esperanza Restaurant and Bar** (☎ 345/948-0531) specializes in local seafood and also serves American dishes. **Mac's Place** (☎ 345/948-0372) offers casual dining.

White Bay

Sonia's Restaurant (☎ 345/948-1214) serves up a variety of dishes. You might also try the air-conditioned **Coral Garden Restaurant** at Brac Reef Beach Resort (☎ 345/948-2265), which features gourmet specialties and local fare in a casual setting.

There's also an outlet for **Domino's Pizza** (☎ 345/948-1266) near West End.

Dawn to Dusk

Beaches

All beaches in the Cayman Islands are public.

Although Brac is notable for its seaside cliffs rather than its beaches, there are a couple of sandy areas. Along with the resort beaches, the Public Beach on the island's south side offers plenty of sunny solitude. Resort beaches are found at Brac Reef Beach Resort.

⚠ WARNING!

Manchineel trees present an unusual danger. These trees, often found near water, have highly acidic leaves and fruit. Rainwater dropping off the leaves can cause painful burns and the tree's tiny, poisonous apples will also burn when stepped on. In most resorts, manchineel trees have been removed or are clearly marked, often with signs and with trunks painted red.

Scuba Diving

Without a doubt, diving is one of the island's top attractions. Over 50 excellent dive sites tempt all levels of divers. The latest attraction is a Russian frigate deliberately sunk in September 1996. Renamed the *M/V Captain Keith Tibbets*, this 330-foot freighter was built for the Cuban navy. It lies approximately 200 yards offshore northwest of Cayman Brac. The bow rests in about 90 feet of water; the stern is just 40 feet below the surface. The sinking of the vessel was recorded by Jean-Michel Cousteau Productions in a documentary film called *Destroyer at Peace*.

Before sinking the vessel, the ship was modified and made safe for divers. Divers can now swim through the upper three decks, although the hull and lower decks cannot be entered. Divers can see into most of the ship, including the missile launcher, fore and aft deck cannons, and living quarters.

It doesn't take long for marine life to discover the additions to their underwater home; already divers have reported spotting eagle rays, stingrays, queen angelfish, filefish, four-eyed butterfly fish, puffer fish, batfish, snapper, red soldier fish, sergeant majors, French grunts, barracuda, jacks, and more.

Best Dive Sites

Anchor Wall

Located on the south side of the island off Dennis Point, this wall dive is considered intermediate level. Don't miss the anchor of an old Spanish galleon; it marks the entrance to a tunnel leading to a vertical wall that drops into the deep blue abyss.

Charlie's Reel

On the north side of the island near Cotton Tree Bay, this 20- to 60-foot dive is a favorite with beginners and is named for a green moray eel who calls this her home.

Inside Out

This wall dive off South East Bay is a favorite with beginners because of its shallow (15- to 50-foot) depth. With coral heads, a tunnel, and plenty of marine life, it's a good choice for anyone.

Radar Reel

Off Half Way Ground on the island's north side, this shallow dive can be reached from shore and is a favorite for night diving. Look for octopus!

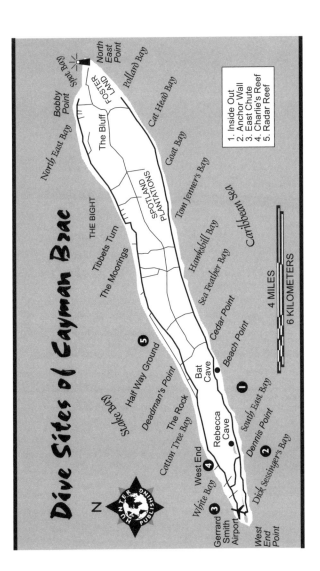

Dive Sites of Cayman Brac

N

1. Inside Out
2. Anchor Wall
3. East Chute
4. Charlie's Reef
5. Radar Reef

North East Point
Spot Bay
Pollard Bay
Bobby Point
FOSTER LAND
North East Bay
The Bluff
Cat Head Bay
Goat Bay
SPOTLAND PLANTATIONS
Tom Jenner's Bay
THE BIGHT
Tibbets Turn
The Moorings
Hawksbill Bay
Sea Feather Bay
Caribbean Sea
Cedar Point
Beach Point
Half Way Ground
Deadman's Point
Bat Cave
The Rock
Cotton Tree Bay
Rebecca Cave
South East Bay
Stake Bay
White Bay
West End
Gerrard Smith Airport
Dennis Point
Dick Sessinger's Bay
West End Point

4 MILES
6 KILOMETERS

HUNTER PUBLISHING

East Chute

This all-level dive, on the north side of the island in White Bay, has something for everyone. Wreck divers will find the remains of a 65-foot vessel in its waters; those looking for spectacular formations will find canyons and tunnels.

Dive & Snorkel Operators

Be sure to pack your "C" card if you plan to scuba dive.

Brac Aquatics Ltd.	☎ 800/544-BRAC
Peter Hughes Dive Tiara	☎ 800/661-DIVE
	☎ 345/948-1553, ext. 129
Reef Divers Brac	☎ 800/327-3835
Reef Beach Resort	

Snorkel trips cost between $10 and $20.

Snorkel Excursions

The wreck of the ***M.V. Capt. Tibbets*** can be enjoyed by snorkelers. Just a short swim from shore, the wreck sits in 50-100 feet of water and is already home to a good selection of marine life.

Fishing

Bonefishing is a top draw for many Cayman Brac vacationers. Guides lead anglers on half- and full-day excursions to seek bonefish in the shallows.

Deep-sea fishing is another popular option and groups of up to four can book a charter for a chance at a trophy catch.

Fishing Guides

Call one of these companies for a fishing guide:

All numbers given are area code 345, unless indicated otherwise.

Capt. Edmund "Munny" Bodden	☎ 948-1228
Shelby Charters	☎ 948-0535
Southern Comfort	☎ 948-1314
Sea Wolf Charters	☎ 948-1066

Unique Tours

Narrated Driving Tour

A good driving tour is available from the National Trust. A 40-minute audio cassette takes visitors on a self-guided drive of the island. You can obtain the tapes from AVIS (☎ 345/948-2847) for a small rental fee or purchase a copy for CI $10 from the Cayman Brac National Trust district committee. ☎ 345/948-2390.

Nature Tours

Birdwatching

Birdwatching is a favorite activity on Cayman Brac. You'll find a self-guided tour at the **Parrot Reserve** (see *Island Sightseeing*, below). There are several other good sites on the island where you might spot the West Indian whistling duck, one of which is the **Saltwater Pond** on the southwest coast.

During the winter months, birders can look for peregrine falcons. Other top birding times are the spring and winter migrations, in February and March as well as November and December. Birders are challenged by about 120 species including the brown booby, Vitelline warbler, and the white-tailed tropicbird. For more information contact Wallace Platts, chairman of the Trust's district committee at ☎ 345/948-2390.

Island Sightseeing

Caves

Cayman Brac's scenic bluff is pocked with caves that frame beautiful seaside views. Some guess that pre-Columbian Indian settlements used the caves; others say they were the lair of plundering pirates who used their dark recesses to hide their loot. During the Great Hurricane of

1932, these caves also offered shelter for many Brackers. Today several of the island's 18 caves have been explored and five are frequently enjoyed by vacationers.

Rebecca's Cave

Located east of Divi Tiara Hotel, this cave is marked with signs. The best-known of the island's caves, sadly this one is named for a young child who died here during the Great Hurricane of 1932.

Peter's Cave

Peter's Cave requires either a climb down a steep path or a hike downhill. From the cave's entrance, travelers can view the community of Spot Bay below.

Other Options

Other challenges for spelunkers include **Skull Cave** (on the north coast near the high school and east of Faith Hospital), two-level **Bat Cave** (on the south side of the island and marked with signs), and, for those prepared for a steep climb, **Great Cave** (on the south side).

❄ **TIP**

If you are interested in doing some caving, bring along a flashlight, a pair of old jeans, and good climbing shoes.

The Brac

The most recognized site on the island is the Brac, the sheer bluff that is visited by hikers and non-hikers alike. To reach the bluff, follow the gravel road north off Ashton Reid Road, the island crossroad. The gravel road runs six miles to a lighthouse. This area is a favorite with birdwatchers. Here, the 180-acre **Parrot Reserve** (page 249) is home to endangered Cayman Brac parrots. Only 400 of the birds remain in the wild on this island.

The Cayman Brac Museum

Hours: Monday through Friday from 9-12 and 1-4 pm and on Saturday from 9-12.
☎ 345/948-2622
Free

This charming museum recalls the early history of seafaring on this island. Located in the former post office, the museum houses ship building tools, photos, and even a replica of a turtle schooner.

Cayman Brac Community Park

On the West End, this park includes a short nature trail that identifies about 10 types of indigenous trees. Dedicated by Governor Michael Gore in 1995, the park is open daily.

Parrot Reserve

The Bluff
Free

Cayman Brac's Parrot Reserve, set atop the Bluff, has a newly opened trail that is open to the public for self-guided tours. The trail is a mile long and takes hikers through the 180-acre Parrot Reserve, home to the endangered Cayman Brac parrot. The best time to spot the emerald green bird is July through September. They're often seen on top of the Bluff as well as around Stake Bay.

The Parrot Reserve is also a good destination for those interested in the flora and fauna of the island. Thirty-eight plant species can be seen here. Look for candlewood, mastic, wild banana orchid plants, and other exotic species.

For more information contact Wallace Platts, chairman of the Trust's district committee at ☎ 345/948-2390.

Shop Til You Drop

Kirk Freeport (☎ 345/948-2612) has a shop on Stake Bay with a selection of duty-free goods. The popular **Grand Cayman Company** (☎ 345/948-1517) also has a duty-free shop at the airport for last-minute jewelry, perfumes, or gift purchases.

Cayman Brac A-Z

Banks

Cayman National Bank has a branch at Tibbetts Square, Cross Road at West End (☎ 345/948-1551).

Credit Cards

Visa, Mastercard, American Express, Diners Club, and Access are commonly accepted at larger establishments; Discover is accepted at some establishments.

Dentists

There's a dental clinic on Cayman Brac; ☎ 345/948-2618.

Emergency Phone Numbers

For medical emergencies, ☎ 911 or 555.

Hospital

Faith Hospital (☎ 345/948-2356), at Stake Bay, has 16 patient beds and an emergency room facility.

Photo Lab

You'll find photo services at **Fast Foto** on Cotton Tree Bay (☎ 345/948-1322). **Cayman Brac Beach Resort** also has an underwater photo shop with rentals, film, and processing on-site.

Room Tax

A 10% government tax is charged on all accommodations. Most hotels add gratuities of 6-10% to this amount.

Tipping

Some restaurants add a 15% gratuity to the bill, so make sure you don't inadvertently tip twice.

Website

You'll find information about Cayman Brac on the Cayman Department of Tourism Website: www.caymanislands.ky.

Appendix

Booklist

Bradley, Patricia. *Birds of the Cayman Islands.* Italy: Caerulea Press, 1995. Natural history and biogeography. Kluwer Academic Publishers, 1995.

Cancelmo, Jesse. *Diving Cayman Islands.* Aqua Quest Publications, Inc. 1997.

Cohen, Shlomo. *Cayman Diver's Guide.* Tel Aviv, Israel Seapen Books, 1990.

Fosdick, Peggy and Sam. *Last Chance Lost?* (story of the Cayman Turtle Farm). Naylor Publishing.

Henderson, James. *Jamaica and the Cayman Islands.* Macmillan Publishing Co., 1996.

O'Keefe, M. Timothy. *Sea Turtles: The Watchers' Guide.* Lakeland, Florida: Larson's Outdoor Publications, 1995.

Permenter, Paris and Bigley, John. *Adventure Guide to the Cayman Islands.* Hunter Publishing, 1997.

Philpott, Don. *Cayman Islands.* NTC Publishing Group, 1996.

Pitcairn, Feodor U. and Hummann, Paul. *Cayman: Underwater Paradise.* Reef Dwellers Press, 1979.

Potter, Betty. *Grand Recipes from the Cayman Islands.* Cayman Islands: Potter Publications, 1985.

Proctor, George, PhD. *Flora of the Cayman Islands.* Balogh Scientific Books.

Raultbee, Paul G., comp. *Cayman Islands.* ABC-CLIO, Inc., 1996.

Roberts, Harry H. *Field Guidebook to the Reefs and Geology of Grand Cayman Island, BWI.* Atlantic Reef Committee, 1977.

Roessler, Carl. *Diving and Snorkeling Guide to the Cayman Islands.* Pisces Publishing Co., 1993.

Sauer, Jonathan D. *Cayman Islands Seashore Vegetation: A Study in Comparative Biogeography.* Books on Demand (University of California Publications in Entomology), 1982.

Smith, Martha. *Cayman Islands: The Beach and Beyond.* Cuchipanda, Inc. 1996.

Wood, Lawson. *Dive Sites of the Cayman Islands.* Passport Books, 1997.

Useful Websites

The Cayman Islands has spawned a wealth of Websites. Throughout the book, we've included Internet addresses for businesses, accommodations, and attractions wherever possible. This appendix includes Websites that offer helpful material about the islands, island activities, and accommodations.

http://www.parisandjohn.com

Check out the authors' Website for information on the latest finds in the Cayman Islands, an e-mail link to tell them about your most recent discoveries, and photos from island excursions.

http://www.oceanfrontiers.com

This site, operated by Ocean Frontiers scuba diving, offers details on dive sites, accommodations, and information specifically for divers. You'll also find a link to weather on the islands. A newsletter has information on recent underwater sightings.

http://www.braclittle.com

Operated by the Brac Reef Resort, Little Cayman Resort and the Conch Club Condominiums, this site has useful information about Little Cayman and Cayman Brac. A newsletter keeps you up to date with changes and offerings at the properties.

http://www.travelfacts.com

This site has pages for a number of Caribbean destinations. Go to the section for the Cayman islands and you'll find a wealth of information, including calendar of events, history, sightseeing and side trips, maps, sports, beaches, other activities, hotel guide, dining guide, shopping, activities, and travel tips.

http://cayman.com

This independent Website has general tourism information.

http://cayman.org

This Website, portions of which are still under development, offers information on transportation, accommodations, what's new, water sports, and a short picture tour of the island.

http://www.candw.ky

Called the "Online Guide to the Cayman Islands," this site (portions still in development) includes information on Aviation Week, banking, diving, entertainment, fishing, getting around, history, island tours, job information, links, recipes, weddings, and weather.

http://www.destination.ky

You can make accommodations reservations online at this site. A neat feature is a WebCam connection to the Turtle Farm so you can see what's going on right now.

http://www.silvanaus.com/travel.htm

This site, called Caribbean Dreams, is operated by Destination Management and Reservations Services. Here you can make online accommodation reservations and get information on dive packages, weddings, and more.

http://www.maintour.com

"Tour the Cayman Islands" offers information on lodging, sports and recreation, attractions, tourism, and more. (Navigate your way to the Cayman Islands section.) Overview sections take a look at the main attractions in each of the tourism areas.

http://ellmer.netmegs.com/cayk.html

"Cayman Islands Scuba Instructions" offer information on wall, reef, night, rebreather, Nitrox and more diving in these islands.

http://www1.netaxs.com/8080.people/ caymans/Cayman_Foods.html

This site has a good overview of the dishes and ingredients of the Cayman Islands along with some recipes.

http://wwwcaymansonline.com

Resources on each of the islands as well as diving, hotels, snorkeling, fishing and more found here.

http://www.diveshop.com/shops/cayman_ island.htm

This site has a long list of dive operators, along with their mailing addresses and phone numbers.

http://www.travel.ky

This Cayman-based site has travel information on each of the Cayman Islands.

http://delta.is.tcu.edu/~FMGoodell/ cayman.html

Links to Cayman history, the turtle farm, banking, hotels/condos, restaurants, nightlife,

Stingray City, Seven Mile Beach, and submarine cruises.

http://www.caymans.net

Information on business services in the Cayman Islands, including accounting firms, banking, captive insurance, company formation, mutual funds, real estate, ship and yacht registration, trustee services, and more.

http://www.cayman-realestate.com/ caymanrealty.html

Learn all you need to know about buying real estate in the Cayman Islands on this site.

http://caribbeansupersite.com/cayman

Learn about shopping, news, business, excursions and the national symbols of these islands on this site.

http://www.caymanport.com/indexx.htm

The Cayman Islands Port Authority operates this site, which includes cruise ship schedules, port business, and attractions; you can also send a Cayman postcard from the site.

http://www.caymanis.com

Duty-free shopping, real estate, banking, tourism and jobs are some of the offerings on this site.

http://www.century21cayman.com

This site has a lot of real estate information and listings for those who are considering Cayman as a first or second home.

http://www.gobeach.com/cayman/

Information on villas, a map of Grand Cayman, travel tips to the Cayman Islands, and more.

http://www.caysail.ky

This page is operated by the Cayman Islands Sailing Club.

http://www.destination.ky

Learn about scuba diving in the Cayman Islands.

http://remaxcayman.com

Along with real estate information and listings, this site has a good newsletter with word on what's happening around Grand Cayman.

http://www.caymanwatersports.com

Information on the Sister Islands, Stingray City, the Cayman Islands International Fishing Tournament, marine conservation, and general facts. You'll also find some specific information if you are considering Cayman as a home: acquisition of permanent residential status, advantages of an offshore financial center, a look at Cayman Islands companies, and more.

Index

Other Books In The ALIVE! Series

ANTIGUA, BARBUDA, ST. KITTS & NEVIS
400 pages $16.95 1-55650-880-8

ARUBA, BONAIRE & CURACAO
340 pages $15.95 1-55650-756-9

BERMUDA
360 pages $15.95 1-55650-844-0

BUENOS AIRES & The Best of Argentina
400 pages $15.95 1-55650-881-6

CANCUN & COZUMEL
332 pages $15.95 1-55650-830-1

JAMAICA
400 pages $15.95 1-55650-882-4

MARTINIQUE, GUADELOUPE, DOMINICA & ST. LUCIA
320 pages $16.95 1-55650-857-3

NASSAU & The Best of The Bahamas
400 pages $15.95 1-55650-883-2

ST. MARTIN & ST. BARTS
320 pages $15.95   1-55650-831-X

VENEZUELA
384 pages $15.95   1-55650-800-X

THE VIRGIN ISLANDS
400 pages $15.95   1-55650-711-9

All Hunter titles are available at bookstores nationwide or from the publisher. To order direct, call 800-255-0343 or send a check plus $3.20 shipping and handling per book to: Hunter Publishing, 130 Campus Drive, Edison, NJ 08818. Secure credit card orders may be made at the Hunter Website, where you'll also find in-depth descriptions of hundreds of travel guides from Hunter.

www.hunterpublishing.com

www.hunterpublishing.com

Hunter's full range of guides to all corners of the globe is featured on our exciting website. You'll find guidebooks to suit every type of traveler, no matter what your budget, lifestyle, or idea of fun.

Adventure Guides – There are now over 40 titles in this series, covering destinations from Costa Rica and the Yucatán to Florida's West Coast, New Hampshire and the Alaska Highway. Complete with information on what to do, as well as where to stay and eat, *Adventure Guides* are tailor-made for the active traveler, focusing on hiking, biking, canoeing, horseback riding, trekking, skiing, watersports, and all other kinds of fun.

Our **Romantic Weekends** guidebooks provide a series of escapes for couples of all ages and lifestyles. Unlike most "romantic" travel books, ours cover more than charming hotels and delightful restaurants, with a host of activities that you and your partner will remember forever.

One-of-a-kind travel books available from Hunter include *Best Dives of the Western Hemisphere; The African-American Travel Guide; Golf Resorts; Chile & Easter Island Travel Companion* and many more.

Full descriptions are given for each book, along with reviewers' comments and a cover image. Books may be purchased on-line via our secure transaction facility.

ADVENTURE GUIDES
from Hunter Publishing

This signature Hunter series targets travelers eager to explore the destination. Extensively researched and offering the very latest information, Adventure Guides are written by knowledgeable authors. The focus is on outdoor activities – hiking, biking, horseback riding, skiing, parasailing, diving, backpacking and waterskiing, among others – and these user-friendly books provide all the details you need, including prices. The best local outfitters are listed, along with contact numbers, addresses, E-mail and Website information. A comprehensive introductory section provides background on history, geography, climate, culture, when to go, transportation and planning. These very readable guides then take a region-by-region approach, plunging into the very heart of each area and the adventures offered, giving a full range of accommodations, shopping, restaurants for every budget, and festivals. Town and regional maps; color photos; fully indexed.

THE ALASKA HIGHWAY
2nd Edition, E & L Readicker-Henderson

"A comprehensive guide.... Plenty of background history and bibliography."
Travel Reference Library on-line

The fascinating highway that passes settlements of the Tlingit and the Haida Indians, with stops at Anchorage, Tok, Skagway, Valdez, Denali National Park and more. Sidetrips and attractions en route, plus details on the Alaska Marine Hwy, Klondike Hwy, Top-of-the-World Hwy. Color photos.

5 x 8 pbk, 400 pp, $16.95, 1-55650-824-7

THE BAHAMAS
2nd Edition, Blair Howard

Fully updated reports for Grand Bahama, Freeport, Eleuthera, Bimini, Andros, the Exumas, Nassau, New Providence Island, plus new sections on San Salvador, Long Island, Cat Island, the Acklins, the Inaguas and the Berry Islands. Mailboat schedules, package vacations and snorkeling trips by Jean-Michel Cousteau.

6 x 9 pbk, 320 pp, $14.95, 1-55650-852-2

EXPLORE BELIZE
4th Edition, Harry S Pariser

"Down-to-earth advice.... An excellent travel guide." – *Library Journal*

Extensive coverage of the political, social and economic history, plus the plant and animal life. Encouraging you to mingle with the locals, Pariser entices you with descriptions of local dishes and festivals. Maps, color.

5 x 8 pbk, 400 pp, $16.95, 1-55650-785-2

CANADA'S ATLANTIC PROVINCES
Barbara Radcliffe Rogers & Stillman Rogers

Pristine waters, rugged slopes, breathtaking seascapes, remote wilderness, sophisticated cities, and quaint, historic towns. Year-round adventures on the Fundy Coast, Acadian Peninsula, fjords of Gros Morne, Viking Trail & Vineland, Saint John River, Lord Baltimore's lost colony. Photos.

5 x 8 pbk, 672 pp, $19.95, 1-55650-819-0

THE CAYMAN ISLANDS
Paris Permenter & John Bigley

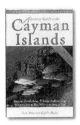

The only comprehensive guidebook to Grand Cayman, Cayman Brac and Little Cayman. Encyclopedic listings of dive/snorkel operators, along with the best sites. Enjoy night-time pony rides on a glorious beach, visit the turtle farms, prepare to get wet at staggering blowholes or just laze on a white sand beach.
Color photos, maps, index.

5 x 8 pbk, 224 pp, $16.95, 1-55650-786-0

THE INSIDE PASSAGE & COASTAL ALASKA
3rd Edition, L & E Readicker-Henderson

"Highly useful." – *Travel Books Review*

Using the Alaska Marine Highway to visit Ketchikan, Bellingham, the Aleutians, Kodiak, Seldovia, Valdez, Seward, Homer, Cordova, Prince of Wales Island, Juneau, Gustavas, Sitka, Haines, Skagway. Glacier Bay, Tenakee. US/Canadian gateway cities profiled.

6 x 9 pbk, 420 pp, $16.95, 1-55650-859-X

COLORADO
Steve Cohen

Adventures in the San Juan National Forest, Aspen, Vail, Mesa Verde National Park, The Sangre de Cristo Mtns, Denver, Boulder, Telluride, Colorado Springs and Durango, plus scores of smaller towns and attractions.
Written by a resident-author.

5 x 8 pbk, 296 pp, $15.95, 1-55680-724-0

COSTA RICA
3rd Edition, Harry S Pariser

"... most comprehensive... Excellent sections on national parks, flora, fauna & history."
– *CompuServe Travel Forum*

Incredible detail on culture, plants, animals, where to stay & eat, as well as practicalities of travel. E-mail and Web site directory.

5 x 8 pbk, 560 pp, $16.95, 1-55650-722-4

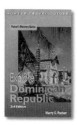

EXPLORE THE DOMINICAN REPUBLIC
3rd Edition, Harry S Pariser

Virgin beaches, 16th-century Spanish ruins, the Caribbean's highest mountain, exotic wildlife, vast forests. Visit Santa Domingo, revel in Sosúa's European sophistication or explore the Samaná Peninsula's jungle. Color photos.

5 x 8 pbk, 340 pp, $15.95, 1-55650-814-X

THE FLORIDA KEYS & EVERGLADES NATIONAL PARK
2nd Edition, Joyce & Jon Huber

"... vastly informative, absolutely user-friendly, chock full of information..."
– Dr. Susan Cropper

"... practical & easy to use."
– *Wilderness Southeast*

Canoe trails, airboat rides, nature hikes, Key West, diving, sailing, fishing. Color.

5 x 8 pbk, 224 pp, $14.95, 1-55650-745-3

FLORIDA'S WEST COAST
Chelle Koster Walton

A guide to all the cities, towns, nature preserves, wilderness areas and white sandy beaches that grace the Sunshine State's western shore. From Tampa Bay to Naples and Everglades National Park to Sanibel Island – it's all here!

5 x 8 pbk, 224 pp, $14.95, 1-55650-787-9

GEORGIA
Blair Howard

"Packed full of information on everything there is to see & do." – *Chattanooga Free Press*

From Atlanta to Savannah to Cumberland Island, this book walks you through antique-filled stores, around a five-story science museum and leads you on tours of old Southern plantations.

5 x 8 pbk, 296 pp, $15.95, 1-55650-782-8

THE GEORGIA & CAROLINA COASTS
Blair Howard

"Provides details often omitted... geared to exploring the wild dunes, the historic districts, the joys... " – *Amazon.com Travel*

Beaufort, Myrtle Beach, New Bern, Savannah, the Sea Islands, Hilton Head and Charleston.

5 x 8 pbk, 288 pp, $15.95, 1-55650-747-X

THE GREAT SMOKY MOUNTAINS
Blair Howard

"The take-along guide." – *Bookwatch*

Includes overlapping Tennessee, Georgia, Virginia and N. Carolina, the Cherokee and Pisgah National Forests, Chattanooga and Knoxville. Scenic fall drives on the Blue Ridge Parkway.

5 x 8 pbk, 288 pp, $15.95, 1-55650-720-8

HAWAII
John Penisten

Maui, Molokai, Lanai, Hawaii, Kauai and Oahu are explored in detail, along with many of the smaller, less-visited islands. Full coverage of the best diving, trekking, cruising, kayaking, shopping and more from a Hawaii resident.

6 x 9 pbk, 420 pp, $15.95, 1-55650-841-7

THE HIGH SOUTHWEST
2nd Edition, Steve Cohen

"Exhaustive detail... [A] hefty, extremely thorough & very informative book."
– *QuickTrips Newsletter*

"Plenty of maps/detail – an excellent guide."
– *Bookwatch*

Four Corners region of Northwestern New Mexico, Soutwestern Colorado, Southern Utah and Northern Arizona. Encyclopedic coverage.

5 x 8 pbk, 376 pp, $15.95, 1-55650-723-2

IDAHO
Genevieve Rowles

Snake River Plain, the Owyhee Mountains, Sawtooth National Recreation Area, the Lost River Range and the Salmon River Mountains. Comprehensive coverage of ski areas, as well as gold-panning excursions and activities for kids, all written by an author with a passion for Idaho.

5 x 8 pbk, 352 pp, $16.95, 1-55650-789-5

JAMAICA
4th Edition, P Permenter & J Bigley

A new edition form authors who have been mingling with the natives for years. The Blue Ridge Mountains, the Rio Grande, Negril River, YS Falls, plus urban destinations such as Montego Bay, Ocho Rios, Negril and Port Antonio. Excursions for budget travelers and big spenders alike! Color photos.

6 x 9 pbk, 360 pp, $16.95, 1-55650-885-9

THE LEEWARD ISLANDS
Antigua, St. Martin, St. Barts, St. Kitts, Nevis, Antigua, Barbuda
Paris Permenter & John Bigley

Far outdistances other guides. Recommended operators for day sails, island-hopping excursions, scuba dives, unique rainforest treks on verdant mountain slopes, and rugged four-wheel-drive trails.

5 x 8 pbk, 248 pp, $14.95, 1-55650-788-7

MAINE
Earl Brechlin

Year-round activities along the coast, up in the mountains and on inland lakes and waterways. Extensive coverage of Acadia, Baxter and Katahdin. Winter delights include skiing, snowmobiling, trekking, ice fishing and snow trekking. Summer offers moonlight swims in secluded lakes.

6 x 9 pbk, 400 pp, $16.95, 1-55650-860-3

MASSACHUSETTS & WESTERN CONNECTICUT
Elizabeth L Dugger

Walking and foliage tours, hiking and biking, kayaking, whalewatching, whitewater rafting, apple-picking festivals and other seasonal treats. Boston, Cape Cod, Nantucket, the Berkshires, Mohawk Trail, Quabbin Reservoir, the Litchfield Hills, along the Housatonic.

6 x 9 pbk, 400 pp, $15.95, 1-55650-861-1

MICHIGAN
Kevin & Laurie Hillstrom

Year-round activities, all detailed here by resident authors. Port Huron-to-Mackinac Island Sailboat Race, Isle Royale National Park, Tour de Michigan cycling marathon. Also: canoeing, dogsledding and urban adventures, including museums and galleries.

5 x 8 pbk, 360 pp, $16.95, 1-55650-820-4

MONTANA
Genevieve Rowles

Flathead and Clearwater Mountains, the Bitterroot Range, Fort Peck Lake, Swan Lake and Glacier National Park are just some of the places Montana offers. Wilderness trips, fly-fishing, Nordic and alpine skiing, rock-hounding, horseback riding, canoeing and more! Stay in a guest ranch, a B&B or a top-class resort – all are profiled.

6 x 9 pbk, 550 pp, $15.95, 1-55650-856-5

NEVADA
Matt Purdue

Adventures throughout the state, from Winnemucca to Great Basin National Park, Ruby Mountain Wilderness to Angel Lake, from Cathedral Gorge State Park to the Las Vegas strip. Take your pick!

6 x 9 pbk, 256 pp, $15.95, 1-55650-842-5

NEW HAMPSHIRE
Elizabeth L Dugger

The Great North Woods, White Mountains, the Lakes Region, Dartmouth & Lake Sunapee, the Monadnock Region, Merrimack Valley and the Seacoast Region. Beth Dugger finds the roads less traveled.

5 x 8 pbk, 360 pp, $15.95, 1-55650-822-0

NORTHERN CALIFORNIA
Lee Foster & Mary Lou Janson

Waves lure surfers to Santa Cruz; heavy snowfall attracts skiers to Lake Tahoe; scuba divers relish Monterey Bay; horseback riders explore trails at Mammoth Lake. Travel the Big Sur and Monterey coasts, enjoy views of Yosemite and savor Wine Country. Resident authors.

5 x 8 pbk, 360 pp, $15.95, 1-55650-821-2

NORTHERN FLORIDA &
THE PANHANDLE
Jim & Cynthia Tunstall

From the Georgia border south to Ocala National Forest and through the Panhandle. Swimming with dolphins and spelunking, plus Rails to Trails, a 47-mile hiking/biking path made of recycled rubber.

5 x 8 pbk, 320 pp, $15.95, 1-55650-769-0

OKLAHOMA
Lynne Sullivan

The only full-sized comprehensive guidebook covering Oklahoma from tip to toe. Explore the rich history of the state's 250,000 Native American residents, their lands and culture, with details on powwows, historical reenactments, and celebrations. The author also tells where, when and how to bike, hike, float, fish, climb, ride and explore, with full information on outfitters and guides. Photos.

6 x 9 pbk, 300 pages, $15.95, 1-55650-843-3

ORLANDO & CENTRAL FLORIDA
Jim & Cynthia Tunstall

Takes you to parts of Central Florida you never knew existed. Tips about becoming an astronaut (the real way and the smart way) and the hazards of taking a nude vacation. Photos and maps throughout.

5 x 8 pbk, 300 pp, $15.95, 1-55650-825-5

THE PACIFIC NORTHWEST
Don & Marjorie Young

Oregon, Washington, Victoria and Vancouver in British Columbia, and California north of Eureka. This region offers unlimited opportunities for the adventure traveler. And this book tells you where to find the best of them.

6 x 9 pbk, 360 pp, $16.95, 1-55650-844-1

PUERTO RICO
3rd Edition, Harry S Pariser

"A quality book that covers all aspects... it's all here & well done."
– *The San Diego Tribune*

"... well researched. They include helpful facts... filled with insightful tips."
– *The Shoestring Traveler*

Crumbling watchtowers and fascinating folklore enchant visitors. Color photos.

5 x 8 pbk, 344 pp, $15.95, 1-55650-749-6

THE SIERRA NEVADA
Wilbur H Morrison & Matt Purdue

California's magnificent Sierra Nevada mountain range. The Pacific Crest Trail, Yosemite, Lake Tahoe, Mount Whitney, Mammoth Lakes, the John Muir Trail, King's Canyon and Sequoia – all are explored. Plus, excellent historical sections. An adventurer's playground awaits!

6 x 9 pbk, 300 pp, $15.95, 1-55650-845-X

SOUTHEAST FLORIDA
Sharon Spence

Get soaked by crashing waves at twilight; canoe through mangroves; reel in a six-foot sailfish; or watch as a yellow-bellied turtle snuggles up to a gator. Interviews with the experts – scuba divers, sky divers, pilots, fishermen, bikers, balloonists, and park rangers. Color photos.

5 x 8 pbk, 256 pp, $15.95, 1-55650-811-5

SOUTHERN CALIFORNIA
Don & Marge Young

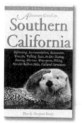

Browse an art festival, peoplewatch at the beach, sportfish near offshore islands and see world-class performances by street entertainers. The Sierras offer a different adventure, with cable cars ready to whisk you to their peaks. A special section covers daytrips to Mexico.

5 x 8 pbk, 400 pp, $16.95, 1-55650-791-7

TEXAS
Kimberly Young

Explore Austin, Houston, Dallas/Ft. Worth, San Antonio, Waco and all the places in-between, from Dripping Springs to Marble Falls. Angle for "the big one" at Highland Lakes, or try some offshore fishing. Tramp through the Big Thicket or paddle on Lake Texoma. Photos throughout.

6 x 9 pbk, 420 pp, $15.95, 1-55650-812-3

TRINIDAD & TOBAGO
2nd Edition, S Pefkaros & K O'Donnell

"Bestselling travel guide." *Amazon.com*

These two unique islands are a delight to explore, with plenty of Caribbean charm. Offering a varied terrain of palm-lined beaches, swamplands, mountains and savannahs, this nation has a wealth of fun opportunities for today's active traveler.

6 x 9 pbk, 320 pp, $16.95, 1-55650-886-7

VERMONT
2nd Edition, Elizabeth L Dugger

Explore the Vermont Valley, Upper Connecticut River Valley, Lake Champlain, the Green Mountains, the Northeast Kingdom, Montpelier. This region offers adventures for every season, from skiing and snowshoeing to swimming, hiking, cycling and canoeing.

6 x 9 pbk, 360 pp, $15.95, 1-55650-887-5

THE VIRGIN ISLANDS
4th Edition, Harry S Pariser

"Plenty of outdoor options.... All budgets are considered in a fine coverage that appeals to readers." – *Reviewer's Bookwatch*

Every island in the Virgins. Valuable, candid opinions. St. Croix, St. John, St. Thomas, Tortola, Virgin Gorda, Anegada. Color.

5 x 8 pbk, 368 pp, $16.95, 1-55650-746-1

VIRGINIA
Leonard M Adkins

The Appalachian Trail winds over the state's eastern mountains. The Great Dismal Swamp offers biking, hiking and canoeing trails, and spectacular wildlife. Skyline Drive and the Blue Ridge Parkway – popular drives in spring and summer. Photos.

5 x 8 pbk, 420 pp, $16.95, 1-55650-816-6

THE YUCATAN
Including Cancún & Cozumel
Bruce & June Conord

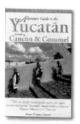

"... Honest evaluations. This book is the one not to leave home without."
– *Time Off Magazine*

"... opens the doors to our enchanted Yucatán."
– Mexico Ministry of Tourism

Maya ruins, Spanish splendor. Deserted beaches, festivals, culinary delights.

5 x 8 pbk, 376 pp, $15.95, 1-55650-792-5

All Hunter titles are available at bookstores nationwide or from the publisher. To order direct, send a check for the total of the book(s) ordered plus $3 shipping and handling to Hunter Publishing, 130 Campus Drive, Edison NJ 08818. Secure credit card orders may be made at the Hunter Web site, where you will also find in-depth descriptions of the hundreds of travel guides we offer.

www.hunterpublishing.com

ORDER FORM

Yes! Send the following *Adventure Guides*:

TITLE	ISBN	PRICE	QTY	TOTAL
			SUBTOTAL	
SHIPPING & HANDLING (United States only) (1-2 books, $3; 3-5 books, $5; 6-10 books, $8)				
		ENCLOSED IS MY CHECK FOR		

NAME:			
ADDRESS:			
CITY:	STATE:	ZIP:	
PHONE: